SOUTH DAKOTA
THE FACE OF THE FUTURE

SOUTH DAKOTA
THE FACE OF THE FUTURE

WILLIAM J. REYNOLDS

CHERBO PUBLISHING GROUP, INC.
ENCINO, CALIF.

ACKNOWLEDGMENTS

For their help, time, and support in the preparation of this book,
my gratitude and appreciation go to these people:

Mr. Doug Murdock, Reference Department, Siouxland Libraries; Mr. Dennis Holub, Executive Director,
South Dakota Arts Council and Acting Director, South Dakota State Library; Ms. Donna Leslie, Communications
Director, South Dakota Retailers Association; Mr. Robert T. Reilly; Ms. Sheila Ring, Membership Services
Coordinator, South Dakota Association of REALTORS; Mr. Ron Robinson; Mr. Tom Troxel, Executive Director,
Black Hills Forest Resource Association; Ms. Maria A. Collis, Editor, Cherbo Publishing Group

DEDICATION

I've often said that my family and I live in South Dakota "on purpose,"
having resided in neighboring states at one time or another;
and so I dedicate this book to the People of South Dakota—
and especially to Peg, Meredith, and Will.

PRESIDENT **Jack C. Cherbo**
EXECUTIVE VICE PRESIDENT **Elaine Hoffman**
EDITORIAL DIRECTOR **Christina M. Beausang**
MANAGING FEATURE EDITOR **Margaret Martin**
FEATURE EDITOR **Maria A. Collis**
ESSAY EDITOR **Tina G. Rubin**
PROFILES EDITORS **Diane M. Ver Steeg, J. Kelley Younger**
PROFILES WRITERS **Brian K. Mitchell, William Schoneberger**
SENIOR PROOFREADER **Sylvia Emrich-Toma**

SENIOR DESIGNER **Mika Toyoura**
CONTRIBUTING DESIGNER **Mary Cameron**
PHOTO EDITOR **Catherine A. Vandenberg**
SALES ADMINISTRATOR **Joan K. Baker**
ACQUISITIONS ADMINISTRATOR **Bonnie J. Aharoni**
PRODUCTION SERVICES MANAGER **Ellen T. Kettenbeil**
ADMINISTRATIVE COORDINATOR **Jahnna Biddle**
REGIONAL DEVELOPMENT MANAGER **Merle Gratton**
PUBLISHER'S REPRESENTATIVES **Dick Fry, Patricia A. Stai**

Cherbo Publishing Group, Inc., Encino, Calif. 91316
© 1999 by Cherbo Publishing Group, Inc.
All rights reserved. Published 1999
Printed in the United States of America

Visit CPG's Web site at www.cherbo-publishing.com.

Library of Congress Cataloging-in-Publication Data
Reynolds, William J.
    A pictorial guide highlighting 20th-century South Dakota
    lifestyle and economic history.
        99-64946
    ISBN 1-882933-28-1

STATE OF SOUTH DAKOTA

OFFICE OF THE GOVERNOR

Dear Reader:

I invite you to join in this celebration of South Dakota. As you rediscover our great state in these pages, you will enjoy the many diverse and interesting roads traveled by our forebears.

Thanks to these settlers and their diverse ways, we enjoy a heritage of variety and risk taking. Our ancestors embraced change. They taught us by doing. Where there was opportunity, they grabbed it. Where there were problems, they fixed them.

This book explores the opportunities, problems, and solutions of our forebears. It reveals the pioneering spirit that formed this state and continues to mold it today. While South Dakota embraces its traditions of agriculture, mining, and tourism, it is grabbing onto new technology and making its own.

Education, health care, and business are all being transformed in South Dakota. Technology is bringing the world to our doorsteps and making neighbors of all South Dakotans.

In this age of change, it is comforting to know that there is one constant you can rely on—South Dakota and her people.

Sincerely,

William J. Janklow

CONTENTS

PROFILES OF CORPORATIONS AND ORGANIZATIONS

The following companies and organizations have made a valuable commitment to the quality of this publication. Cherbo Publishing Group gratefully acknowledges their participation in *South Dakota: The Face of the Future*.

ESSAYISTS

SOUTH DAKOTA HIGHLIGHTS

AREA: 77,116 square miles
POPULATION: 737,973 (1997 est.)
CAPITAL: Pierre
MOTTO: "Under God the People Rule"
STATEHOOD: Admitted as the 40th state
   simultaneously with North Dakota, the 39th state, on November 2, 1889
BIRD: Chinese ring-necked pheasant
FLOWER: Pasque
NICKNAMES: Mount Rushmore State, Coyote State

PEOPLE

GEORGE "SPARKY" ANDERSON (b. 1934), born in Bridgewater, is the only manager in major league history to win the World Series in both the American and National Leagues.

GERTRUDE SIMMONS BONNIN (Zitkala-Sa, 1876–1938), Sioux writer and pan-Indian activist, published two book-length collections, *Old Indian Legends* and *American Indian Stories,* and founded the National Council of American Indians.

TOM BROKAW (b. 1940), anchor of *NBC Nightly News,* was born in Webster and got his broadcasting start in Yankton.

MARTHA "CALAMITY JANE" CANARY BURKE (1852–1903), originally from Missouri, is said to have nursed Deadwood's miners through an outbreak of smallpox in 1878. She was an expert horse-woman and sharpshooter, an army scout and Indian fighter, a pony express rider, and Wild Bill Hickok's sweetheart. Her advice: "Never go to bed sober, alone, or with a red cent left in your pocket."

JOSEPH J. "JOE" FOSS (b. 1915), a Sioux Falls native, downed 26 enemy planes in World War II. He received the Congressional Medal of Honor and went on to become commander of the state's Air National Guard, a two-term governor, the first commissioner of the American Football League, and president of the National Rifle Association.

CHARLES D. "SAM" GEMAR (b. 1955), NASA astronaut, was born in Yankton. Gemar has flown on three space shuttle missions, logged over 580 hours off-planet, and reports that the Great Lakes of South Dakota can be seen from space.

OSCAR HOWE (1915–1983) portrayed the life and heritage of his people, the Yanktonai Sioux, through his arrestingly vibrant and powerful paintings. His murals grace the interior of the Mitchell Corn Palace.

ERNEST ORLANDO LAWRENCE (1901–58), 1939 Nobel Prize–winner in physics, was born in Canton. One of the architects of the atomic age, Lawrence invented a circular accelerator, or cyclotron, which smashes atoms, releasing particles for use in research. The chemical element lawrencium is named for him.

GEORGE MCGOVERN (b. 1922) won the Distinguished Flying Cross as a World War II bomber pilot. He represented South Dakota in both houses of Congress for a total of 22 years between 1957 and 1981, and ran for president against Richard Nixon in 1972.

BILLY MILLS (Makata Taka Hela, b. 1938), a Sioux from Pine Ridge, captured a gold medal in the 1964 Tokyo Olympics in the 10,000-meter run, the only American ever to win that event. Mills's life was the subject of the film *Running Brave.* He currently serves as national spokesperson for Running Strong for American Indian Youth.

ALLEN "AL" NEUHARTH (b. 1924) grew up in Eureka, where he worked summers on his grandfather's ranch. He graduated from harvesting cow chips to herding cattle before going on to become chairman of Gannett, the largest media company in the United States, and to found *USA Today,* a national newspaper with a circulation of about six million.

PAT O'BRIEN (b. 1948), journalist and *CBS Sports* personality, was born in Sioux Falls and graduated from the University of South Dakota.

TERRY REDLIN (b. 1937) was named America's most popular gallery artist, 1991–1998, by *U.S. ART* magazine. His landscapes and wildlife paintings and prints can be seen on everything from

collector plates to postage stamps. He is also an active conservationist.

LAURA INGALLS WILDER (1867–1957) set her books *By the Shores of Silver Lake* and *Little Town on the Prairie* in the area near De Smet, where she lived as a teenager with her homesteader parents.

DID YOU KNOW?

The State of South Dakota has had a balanced budget for 109 years.

Of major midwestern cities, Sioux Falls has the second lowest cost of living, with a composite index of 94.9.

South Dakota appears in the top 10 on virtually every list of crop or livestock production; it ranks first in oats and hay and second in rye, flaxseed, and sunflower seeds.

South Dakota's high school graduation rate is nearly 90 percent, the highest in the nation.

South Dakota has the lowest student-to-computer ratio in the United States—3.8 to one, compared to the national rate of 7.3 to one.

South Dakota claims the geographic center of the United States, a point 21 miles north of Belle Fourche.

The U.S. government's central archives for nonmilitary satellite images and aerial photography are kept at the Earth Resources Observation Systems (EROS) Data Center, near Baltic. EROS distributes this data to scientists worldwide.

According to *The Guinness Book of World Records,* the greatest variance in temperature occurred in the Black Hills, in 1943. First, thermometers in Spearfish registered four degrees below zero. Then the temperature rose 49 degrees—in less than two minutes!

More than 6,000 musical instruments from all over the world find their home in the unique Shrine to Music Museum, on the University of South Dakota campus in Vermillion. The collection includes a 1785 French harpsichord, a nine-foot-tall slit drum from the South Pacific, and one of only two known Antonio Stradivari guitars remaining in the world.

MEMORABLE MOMENTS IN SOUTH DAKOTA HISTORY

1863: The Homestead Act goes into effect in the Dakota territory. Men and women can now claim 160 acres of land for little more than a token sum and the determination to live there for five years.

1874: The Black Hills gold rush is sparked by a story in a Chicago newspaper reporting that Lieutenant General George Armstrong Custer has found gold on the banks of French Creek.

1889: South Dakota is the first state to be admitted simultaneously to the Union with another state—North Dakota. (Today the states are ranked alphabetically by agreement.)

1927: Construction begins on Mount Rushmore. The sculpture will be completed 14 years later.

1948: South Dakota becomes the leading gold producer in the United States.

1956: Fort Randall Dam is dedicated on the Missouri River. It is the first of four dams planned in accordance with the Flood Control Act of 1944. These dams will create the Great Lakes of South Dakota.

1968: South Dakota State University professors Aelred Kurtenbach and Duane Sander launch Daktronics, Inc., whose scoreboards and computer-programmed displays are now seen by millions of people in more than 50 countries every day.

1974: Mammoth Site, one of the largest displays of fossil mammoths ever found, is discovered by accident during construction of a Hot Springs housing project.

1980s: Citibank transfers its credit card processing operation from New York to South Dakota, becoming the first of many credit card and commercial banking concerns to locate or expand here.

1986: Toshiba is the first Japanese company to invest in South Dakota when it opens a production facility in Mitchell.

1990: A small company called Gateway 2000 relocates to South Dakota. Today Gateway is a globally recognized leader in the personal computer industry.

FIRSTS AND INNOVATIONS FROM THE MOUNT RUSHMORE STATE

1897: South Dakota is the first state to pass initiative and referendum legislation in the House and Senate, giving voters the power to propose laws and submit them to popular vote.

1905: Amanda Clement of Hudson becomes the first professional woman

umpire, calling the shots for semipro baseball teams in five midwestern states.

1910: Thomas Fawick of Sioux Falls builds America's first four-door car, the Fawick Flyer.

1930: Ernest O. Lawrence, a Canton native, invents the cyclotron, which remains the single most important tool in high-energy physics and is also used in medical research and treatment.

1935: The *Explorer 11* balloon ascends from Rapid City to a record height of 72,394 feet and produces the country's first photographs showing the curvature of the earth and the division between the atmosphere and stratosphere.

1958: Brookings becomes the first U.S. city to have fluorescent lighting installed on every street in compliance with engineering codes.

1974: The first Super 8 Motel opens in Aberdeen. Today there are more than 1,600 Super 8 Motels in the United States and Canada.

1996: Ground breaks in Mitchell on the world's first archeodome, designed to enable year-round excavation and research of a 1,000-year-old Native American village.

1997: Gateway 2000 becomes the first company on the planet to receive an extraterrestrial order when cosmonauts aboard the *Mir* space station purchase two G6-233 Pentium II personal computer systems on line.

1999: Governor Bill Janklow announces a $7 million program to link all South Dakota schools to one another through video conferencing technology.

PART ONE　INFINITELY VARIED

If South Dakota did not exist, it would be necessary to invent it. Imagine a place simultaneously pastoral and untamed. A place that is at once rustic and sophisticated. A place rooted firmly in the past—one of the last outposts of the great American frontier—yet thrusting resolutely into the twenty-first century.

Imagine a place of breathtaking mountains and unspoiled grasslands; lush, verdant forests and immeasurably rich mines and quarries; the most desolate badlands and the most luxuriant farmlands—all reposing beneath a placid azure sky that, seemingly without warning, may explode into the most ferocious displays of Mother Nature's capricious temperament and incontestable might.

Imagine one of the largest states in the Union with one of the smallest populations. Imagine arctic winters and Saharan summers alternating with delightful springs and achingly beautiful autumns. Imagine a state more than 90 percent farmland being also one of the fastest growing venues of finance, technology, health care, and entrepreneurship.

Imagine. . . . Ah, but you don't have to imagine. South Dakota does exist, and if it sounds too good to be true, then it must be the exception that proves the rule. Sometimes something that sounds too good to be true is both true *and* too good to be true.

Welcome to that place. Welcome to a land of limitless possibilities, limitless surprises. Welcome to the Mount Rushmore State—South Dakota.

Badlands National Park contains 65 million years of paleontological and human history, from prehistoric mammoths to bison—each with their respective hunters—to the Oglala Sioux living there today.

CHAPTER ONE

LAND OF MOUNTAINS, LAKES, AND PRAIRIES

Part of the beauty of South Dakota is that it affords one the opportunity to choose among several South Dakotas,

each with its own unique qualities and characteristics. From towering mountains in the west to crystal blue lakes

in the center to flowing prairie in the east; from Wild West terrains to four-star dining; from Badlands to grass-

lands—all are available within the 77,116 square miles that are the Mount Rushmore State.

This near-infinite variety is a wonderful thing for those lucky enough to live here, but because it can be a bit overwhelming, it is helpful to think in terms of three broad features that define the landscape: the Black Hills, the Badlands, and farmland.

THE HILLS

The Black Hills, in extreme western South Dakota, have been called "the heart of everything that is." Sacred to Native American peoples in both ancient and modern times, "the Hills," as they are colloquially known, are in fact mountains. Indeed, Harney Peak, the highest point in the Hills at 7,242 feet, is considered the highest mountain between the Rockies and the Alps. Some 2.7 million visitors a year flock to that world-renowned Black Hills "shrine to democracy," Mount Rushmore National Memorial. But the story of the Hills did not begin, nor does it end, with Mount Rushmore.

The Hills today are perhaps South Dakota's strongest link to its frontier heritage, those Old West days when Wild Bill Hickok and Calamity Jane and their confreres trod the unpaved streets of Deadwood and Lead and the

other towns that sprang up during the last great gold rush in American history.

Even the formation of the Hills was wild. Some 35 or 40 million years ago this was a marshy plain. Over the course of another 14 million years, terrible, overwhelming forces below the earth's surface heaved molten matter skyward, transforming the marsh into this great dark cathedral that the Indian people would much later dub *Paha Sapa*—"hills that are black."

THE BADLANDS

If the Black Hills tower as a cathedral above the plains, then perhaps the White River Badlands are indeed as George Armstrong Custer described them: "hell with the fire burned out." Roughly 90 miles east of the Hills, the Badlands are a byproduct of the same geological turmoil. The Badlands had once not been land at all, but rather a great salt sea. Over nameless

Mount Rushmore was not the original Black Hills site planned for Gutzon Borglum's monument. And the faces were first envisioned as those of Lewis and Clark and other legends of the Old West.

PHOTO: © Tom Till

ages, the sea became a marsh, and home to such prehistoric peculiarities as saber-toothed tigers, three-toed horses, and mammoths. But the energies that thrust the peaks of the Black Hills heavenward buried the marsh in sand, silt, and ash. Erosion—and the centuries—took it from there, carving out this vest-pocket Grand Canyon, which French-Canadian trappers, the first non-Indians in the neighborhood, called *les mauvaises terres à traverser*— "bad lands to travel across." Eerily beautiful, both bleak and serene, the Badlands today are not merely a popular stop but also a virtual gold mine for paleontologists, geologists, and anyone else who longs to unearth the secrets of the planet's prehuman history.

THE FARMLAND

Farther east, one inevitably encounters "the river"—the Missouri River—which raggedly halves the state as it

In the late 1800s entire South Dakota towns pulled up stakes to move closer to new railroad lines and the settlers and commerce they brought. Many communities that stayed put became prairie ghost towns, such as this one at Okaton.

makes its seemingly capricious way from southern Montana across the Dakotas and on down to its rendezvous with the Mississippi near St. Louis. The Missouri does more than split the state into two more or less equal halves: It bisects the very culture of South Dakota, forming a kind of spiritual line of demarcation between the rough-hewn frontier flavor of "West River" South Dakota and the no less ruggedly individualistic but considerably more pastoral ambience of "East River" South Dakota.

When folks elsewhere hear the name South Dakota, they probably envision the farmland of the eastern, and

FACING PAGE: *Spearfish Canyon is still as unspoiled as when Sioux and Cheyenne Indians speared fish in the creek. Kevin Costner shot several scenes for his film* Dances with Wolves *in this area.*

especially the southeastern, portion of the state. Here are the verdant, gently rolling plains, the "miles and miles of miles and miles" that passers-through complain about but which contain some of the most fertile and productive farmland in the world. Because this end of the state is so different from the other, it comes as no shock that it was created in a wholly different fashion. The landscape of the west was formed largely by subterranean energies pushing upward, but the topography of the east was created by southward-migrating glaciers grinding the terrain

into a nearly flat prairie. The retreating glaciers left behind a number of gifts: lakes, granite suitable for quarrying, and rich, black topsoil.

Given the West River–East River dichotomy, it has been suggested many times that Congress would have done better to have divided Dakota Territory the long way back in 1889, hacking out tall, narrow East Dakota and West Dakota rather than North and South. Logical, but think of all the variety that would have been lost!

BELOW: *The Great Plains bison, once 60 million strong, were nearly extinct by 1900. Today 1,500 bison roam 73,000-acre Custer State Park, thanks to forward thinkers such as rancher James "Scotty" Philip (1857–1911) who started with 80 bison and built a herd of 1,000.*

CHAPTER TWO

A GOOD LIFE

Variety of landscape is one thing, but in the course of daily living, true variety comes from people, from the constant interweaving of cultures, ideas, and experiences that creates a strong and colorful social fabric. South Dakota can trace its confluence of peoples at least as far back as 1775, when French Canadian fur trader Pierre Dorion stopped on his way up the Missouri River from St. Louis. He met a Sioux woman near present-day

Yankton and married into her tribe. Years later Dorion would serve as a Sioux interpreter for Meriwether Lewis and William Clark as they passed through South Dakota en route to the Pacific.

More than 90 percent of today's South Dakotans are of European stock, most of them with roots in Scandinavia, Germany, Eastern Europe, or Ireland. A good many of these people are descendants of the brave and hardy Dakota Territory homesteaders who came in the late 1800s to carve a living and a life out of the vast, unrelenting prairie. More than 50,000 Native Americans comprise the state's next largest ethnic group.

While the history of Native Americans and whites in South Dakota is not exactly an exemplar of harmonious race relations, an expressed spirit of reconciliation between the races has been active across the state for at least a decade. Indeed, in that spirit, Columbus Day and Native American Day are celebrated together in South Dakota. In recent years people of color have joined the mix as well. Today it is not unusual to find Laotian, Vietnamese, Ethiopian, and Jamaican names in the telephone directories of many South Dakota cities and towns.

What brings these folks here? And what keeps all of them here? Certainly there are as many answers as there are South Dakotans—about 750,000. But in general they appreciate what is inevitably referred to as "quality of life"—good environment; good economy; and the time, means, and health to enjoy them.

HEALTH, WEALTH, AND HAPPINESS

Where health is concerned, South Dakota has over 2,000 doctors and 60 licensed hospitals providing the second highest number of hospital beds per 1,000 people in the United States. The state has the lowest incidence of AIDS cases in the nation.

And South Dakotans have the means to enjoy their good health. Although much is made of low wages in South Dakota, "real annual pay"—adjusted for inflation and environmental factors—rose 5.1 percent through the 1990s, compared to only 2.2 percent for the nation as a whole.

THIS PAGE: *Sioux Falls, South Dakota's largest city, has been ranked among the most livable in the nation.* FACING PAGE: *A centuries-old tradition of handiwork went into this Dakotah dancer's costume for his performance at the Fort Sisseton Historical Festival.*

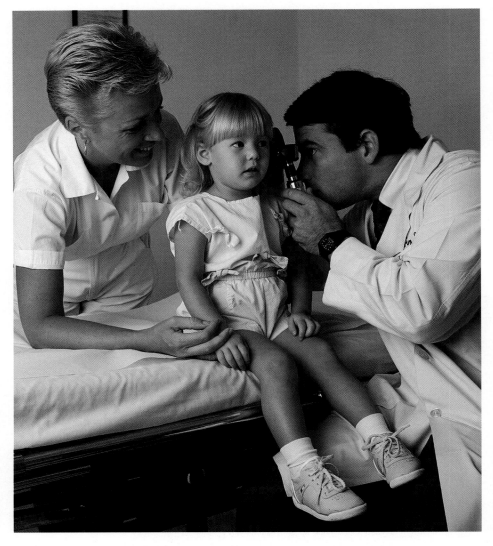

Council's 1997 "Report Card on American Education," South Dakota leads the nation in high school graduations (88.7 percent compared to 68.8 percent nationally) and is fifth in both ACT and SAT scores. Why? Parent involvement is generally high, as is school attendance—sort of a juvenile spin on the renowned midwestern work ethic. That ethic, naturally, imbues the staff and administration of most schools, too: South Dakota has one of the lowest teacher salary rates in the United States, but most schools have little trouble finding and retaining teachers, which bespeaks of dedication to their vocation. Business and industry play a part, too. For example, Sioux Falls public schools enjoy interesting and mutually beneficial "business partnerships" with various entities in the city, from banks to retirement homes. Yet South Dakota's expenditures per pupil, at just over $4,000 a year, are among the lowest in the United States.

The cost of living is relatively low, with a composite index of 94.9 in Sioux Falls, compared to 100.4 and 99.1 for nearby Minneapolis and Des Moines, respectively. There is no personal income tax, no personal property tax, and a mere 4 percent state sales tax. So there may be some truth to the local quip that South Dakotans earn less but keep more than their neighbors.

It is also less likely that someone will steal what they have. South Dakota has the 44th lowest crime rate in the nation. The state ranks no higher than 39th in any particular type of crime—violent crime, robbery, etc.—and has the nation's lowest incidence of motor vehicle thefts. The police don't recommend it, but there are still communities in South Dakota where people seldom lock their doors.

BOOK LEARNING

Perhaps the low crime rate is a result of high educational quality. According to the American Legislative Exchange

In higher education, more than a dozen colleges and universities serve the state. They are joined by a number of vocational-technical schools, community colleges, and business and trade schools. Augustana College, in Sioux Falls, consistently finds itself among the top 10 midwestern liberal arts colleges as ranked by *U.S. News & World Report*.

FORESIGHT

And the picture looks good for the future. Although agriculture is undergoing one of its periodic downturns as the century draws to a close, the rest of the economy is generally strong and, perhaps more important, diversifying. South Dakota's population grew some 6 percent in the 1990s. The manufacturing sector alone, which employs roughly 50,000 people, gained more than 15,000 jobs during that same period. Companies such as Citibank, 3M, Gateway, and Toshiba have made homes in South Dakota, polishing the state's growing image as a center for finance, electronics, and commerce as well as cash crops and heads carved in rock. This is a good place to start a business, too. The 1998 Small Business Survival Index rated South Dakota best in the nation for an economic environment that fosters entrepreneurship. No wonder the unemployment rate in early 1998 was a mere 2.7 percent, compared to 4.3 percent nationally.

No wonder, too, that people in South Dakota are so— well, there is no way to say it without it sounding like a cliché—*nice.* Folks around here are nice. Everybody comments on it. Sure, there is that midwestern reserve, that closemouthed, size-it-up-first attitude that newcomers may find off-putting. But after all, there are only about nine people for every one of South Dakota's 77,116 square miles, so they are just not all that used to rubbing elbows. They tend to be a little more introspective, maybe. A little more reserved. A little more considerate of people's personal space. Except, perhaps, during one small interval in the year: the high school basketball tournaments.

Aberdeen's Northern State University specializes in preparing students to compete in the global marketplace, with courses in international finance, marketing, and management. NSU's internship program benefits both students and the local business community.

CHAPTER THREE

FUN, SOUTH DAKOTA—STYLE

At first glance, it may seem that there is less to do in South Dakota than in other states. And it is probably true that more densely populated states, such as near neighbors Minnesota and Colorado, offer more in sheer quantity of diversions. Yet tourism is South Dakota's second largest industry. Wonder why? Don't bother asking South Dakotans. Most don't give it much thought. They are much too busy getting out and having fun.

THE SPORTING LIFE

South Dakotans are no different than anyone else in the United States in their collective love of sports. There are no major league professional sports here, but that is quite all right with the local population. The Vikings, the Broncos, and the Packers; the Twins and the Royals; the Timberwolves and the Nuggets—all enjoy near-fanatical devotion from the Mount Rushmore State. And minor league professional and semipro sports have gained a foothold in recent years. The Sioux Falls Canaries are a recent reincarnation of an early twentieth-century baseball team, and are one of the top-ranked teams in the independent Northern League. The Sioux Falls Skyforce, meanwhile, has in its short history become one of the winningest teams in the Continental Basketball Association, which also boasts the top-notch Rapid City Thrillers.

Attempts to launch hockey and football franchises are under way as well. One such proposal has the fledgling Indoor Football League (IFL) in negotiations with the Sioux Falls Arena. The IFL, a minor league version of the Arena Football League, has expressed its hopes to mount a Sioux Falls team by the 2000 season. And the

Sioux Falls Stampede should bring hockey fans to the Sioux Falls Arena in the very near future.

Youth sports are favored, too. After all, South Dakota is the birthplace of American Legion Baseball, and nearly every town across the state seems to have American Legion or Babe Ruth teams—or both.

But it is really college and high school athletics that dominate the local sporting scene. Virtually every conceivable sport is locally represented, but traditionally basketball has claimed the most attention, especially high school basketball. In March, everything else is pretty much put on hold until the schools have thrashed it out in the state basketball tournaments.

THIS PAGE: *The state department of tourism estimates that Missouri River recreation has an economic impact of $165 million a year, about half of it from fishing.* FACING PAGE: *In 1939, Korczak Ziolkowski, an assistant to Gutzon Borglum at Mount Rushmore, got a letter from Chief Henry Standing Bear saying that the Sioux "would like the white man to know the red man has great heroes, too." Seven years later Ziolkowski began work on the world's largest statue under construction—563 feet high and 641 feet long—a monument to the Sioux warrior Crazy Horse (1849–1877).*

FACING PAGE: *Half jackrabbit, half antelope, the "jackalope" welcomes riders outside Wall Drug. Signs indicating the mileage to Wall Drug have popped up all over the world, including at a train station in Kenya, at the North Pole, on Mount Fuji, and near the Eiffel Tower and the Taj Mahal. Also, American soldiers can usually be counted on to post homemade signs wherever they are stationed.*

Whoever coined the phrase "March Madness" didn't know the half of it! However, South Dakotans are basically back to their normal, nice selves by early April.

THE GREAT INDOORS

After basketball, the big indoor activity is shopping. The Empire/Empire East in Sioux Falls is reputed to be the biggest retailing shrine between Denver and Minneapolis. With such national powerhouses as the Disney Store, Eddie Bauer, and Sears rubbing elbows with regional giants such as Dayton's, Younkers, and Musicland as well as the eclectic assortment of local stores, booths, and eateries, a shopper can keep occupied for a good long time.

But eventually even the most devoted of shoppers looks for other diversions. South Dakota offers plenty. Rapid City, on the western edge of the state, and Sioux Falls, in the southeastern corner, attract major entertainment, especially pop, rock, and country acts. Both cities are rapidly emerging centers for the arts, with museums and galleries expanding—or springing up outright—in and around both. Sioux Falls, for example, recently completed the conversion of a huge, disused downtown high school into the Washington Pavilion of Arts and Science, which boasts a state-of-the-art performance center, a large-format movie theater, a hands-on science museum, galleries, classrooms, and office space for arts organizations.

Opportunities abound in smaller venues, too. Watertown is justifiably proud of native son Terry Redlin, one of the country's most popular wildlife artists, who in turn thinks highly enough of his hometown to have built his Redlin Art Center there, housing more than 100 of his original paintings. South Dakota State University, in Brookings, is host to a collection of works by Harvey Dunn, another native, whose illustrations and paintings graced the *Saturday Evening Post* and other major magazines in the early part of this century. There is a memorial to Laura Ingalls Wilder in De Smet, where she spent much of her childhood, and where the Ingalls house and other landmarks have been lovingly preserved.

And there is more: "The World's Only Corn Palace," at Mitchell. Al's Oasis at Chamberlain, with its western-themed gallery and restaurant. The world-famous Wall Drug, at the town of Wall on the extreme edge, or "wall," of the Badlands. The casinos and historic venues of Deadwood, Lead, Custer, and other towns dotting the Black Hills. Theaters, galleries, museums, or all of the above at virtually every college or university.

It is just impossible to run out of things to do—and the world outside offers still more.

THE GREAT OUTDOORS

A master of understatement would say that South Dakota is an outdoor-lover's paradise. More than one million acres of western South Dakota alone are given over to national parks, forests, grasslands, memorials, and monuments. State parks preserve additional acres there and across the state. Camping, hiking, biking, climbing, horseback riding, skiing, swimming, boating—all these activities and more take place in the Black Hills, on the four South Dakota Great Lakes formed by dams along the Missouri River, or in the environs of the glacial lakes of the northeast.

Hunting and fishing are forces to be reckoned with: Walleye, smallmouth and largemouth bass, bullhead, yellow perch, and northern pike are only a few of the finned critters that vie for the hook in the various lakes and rivers of the state. Hunters from all over the world arrive in South Dakota every fall for the opening of pheasant season, but the state is also known for goose and duck, white-tailed deer, fox and coyote, and other, smaller furbearing game.

BUT WAIT, THERE'S MORE!

What about fairs and festivals, parades and pageants, those too-numerous-to-count events and opportunities found in every corner of the state, at every time of year? One could head to White for the annual Pioneer Days, immersing oneself in such nineteenth-century-inspired activities as a hot dog/ice cream social, parade, and beanbag tournament. Or go prowling for antiques in Canton. Or celebrate the achievements of Lewis and Clark at Chamberlain's Lewis and Clark Historic Festival. Or kick up one's heels at the Corn Palace Polka Festival in Mitchell. Or investigate any of scores of county fairs, sidewalk art shows, powwows, historic tours, and more.

This is South Dakota: The possibilities are endless!

CENTRAL PLAINS
ACROSS THE WIDE MISSOURI

NORTHEAST
GIFTS OF THE GLACIERS

WEST
THE HEART OF EVERYTHING THAT IS

RING-NECKED PHEASANT

SOUTHEAST
THE WILD, WILD EAST

PASQUE
FLOWER

PART TWO

GREAT FACES, GREAT PLACES

If there is an almost limitless number of South Dakotas from which to choose, there is also a virtually unlimited number of ways in which to look at the state, to view and consider and understand it. At its simplest, you have West River and East River—in general, ranch land and farmland. But then there are the colorful variations in landscape and lifestyle that defy this two-sided view. There is the west, a tourist's dream, taking in the thickly forested Black Hills and the stark White River Badlands. The central plains region, which straddles the Missouri River and the Great Lakes of South Dakota, contains the seat of state government. Carved by glaciers and dotted with farms, the northeast is now also known as a cultural center. In the southeast you will find the archetypal Midwest prairie, plus South Dakota's largest city, oldest university, and some of its most exciting developments in health care, finance, and high technology.

How many states are being discussed here? Just the one, the ever-surprising Mount Rushmore State—always more than the sum of its parts.

CHAPTER FOUR

THE WEST: THE HEART OF EVERYTHING THAT IS

In some respects, western South Dakota is where the state's past and future intersect. On the one hand, there is the unspoiled openness of this region, especially evident when one stands at "the heart of everything that is," the Black Hills. One doesn't have to be a Native American to intuitively understand the sacredness of the place; one doesn't have to be a "West Riverite;" one doesn't even have to be a South Dakotan. One need only stand and

gaze across these peaks, across the dense forests of Black Hills spruce (the state tree), Norway pine, and other conifers that make the mountains appear black. It is amazingly easy here to imagine that you are the first person ever to stand where you stand.

On the other hand, one stands in the second fastest growing region of the state. The Rapid City area trails only greater Sioux Falls in population growth and its concomitant urbanization and worldliness. One stands also in the thick of South Dakota's second largest industry, tourism. Although the tourism industry is a large pie, with each region enjoying its own slice, western South Dakota claims the lion's share. Millions of people a year make the pil-

grimage to the Hills, to Mount Rushmore and the nearby Crazy Horse monument, to the Wild West ambience of such gold rush towns as Lead and Deadwood, generating roughly $1 billion in economic activity.

And so one stands at the crossroads of time, where the past is alive. The Black Hills are as sacred to Native American people today as they were before the first white people ever got up the nerve to try a transatlantic voyage. That alone forms an unbreakable bridge to the past, a

bridge buttressed by the fact that tourism here depends largely on that Old West ambience, on the living ghosts of Wild Bill Hickok, Calamity Jane, Sitting Bull, George Armstrong Custer, and all the other larger-than-life figures of a past that will live forever, even as a vital and exciting future unfolds.

THE LAST GOLD RUSH

Perhaps nowhere is the past more evident than in the rustic, picturesque towns that dot the Black Hills, towns whose oddly romantic names connote those heady, lawless Wild West days: Deadwood, Lead, Custer, Hill City, Keystone, and others.

Deadwood was a product of gold fever. Custer discovered gold in the Black Hills in 1874. By 1876 some 25,000 souls had flocked to Deadwood. Many were miners. Some were legitimate merchants hoping to build a business in a booming town. But there were also the madams, the cardsharps, the con artists, and the outlaws, all of whom contributed to Deadwood's reputation as one of the

FACING PAGE: *Lush green enclaves spread among the obelisks in Badlands National Park. Labelled* mako sica, *or "land bad," by the Lakota people, this land of contrasts covers 244,000 acres.*

ABOVE: *The Sturgis Rally and Races attracts more than 100,000 motorcycle enthusiasts to the Black Hills every August—including such celebrities as "easy rider" Peter Fonda, Emilio Estevez, and Neil Diamond. Nearby, in the National Motorcycle Museum and Hall of Fame, is a 1907 Harley-Davidson reputed to be the oldest unrestored, running Harley in the world.*

rowdiest mining camps in the West. Many historic buildings from the late 1800s are still preserved in Deadwood, including Saloon No. 10, where Wild Bill Hickok was gunned down. These days, casino gambling has been restored in Deadwood, and visitors also want to see such glittering new gaming palaces as the Midnight Star.

An even bigger gold rush player was Lead. Its name rhymes with "seed" and refers to a vein of gold, the Homestake Lead, discovered in 1876 and still mined

today. The Homestake Mine is the largest gold mine in the Western Hemisphere, and South Dakota is the nation's second leading gold producer.

The biggest community in the Hills, and the second biggest in the state, Rapid City did not spring out of the gold rush—at least not directly. The city was founded by disenchanted miners who decided to try their hand at commerce. The community grew, and with the arrival of the railroad in 1886, its future was assured. Still the area's commercial center, Rapid City leads the region in health care, finance, and retailing, as well as businesses related to mining, lumbering, agriculture, and tourism. The four-

FACING PAGE: *"Indian Joe" Whiting maintains a respectful distance from Bear Butte, the 1,400-foot volcanic bubble sacred to Plains Indians and enshrined today in a 2,000-acre state park.*

square-block Rushmore Plaza Civic Center hosts all manner of events from rock concerts to rodeos, while the South Dakota Air and Space Museum at Ellsworth Air Force Base displays everything from General Eisenhower's personal B-25 transport to a model of a stealth bomber.

Another Black Hills community whose origin is only peripherally related to the gold rush is Hot Springs. This was a popular spa and health resort in the 1800s, but since 1974 Hot Springs has been famous as the location of Mammoth Site, where the remains of more than 40 of these Pleistocene-era gargantua have been uncovered. Mammoth Site is the only *in situ* (bones left as found) display of fossil mammoths in America, and one of the largest such discoveries ever.

Barroom brawls, fortunes lost at the card table or in a back alley; men and women made and unmade by fate: everyday occurrences in the boomtowns of the late 1800s. Now a quaint tourist stop, Rockerville's reconstructed main street hints at a storied past.

MEN OF STONE

Mammoths notwithstanding, most people visit the Black Hills to see something created more recently: Mount Rushmore National Memorial. Mount Rushmore was not sculptor Gutzon Borglum's first choice for a monumental carving. Nor is today's massive sculpture what he had in mind when he began construction in 1927. In addition to ordinary design changes, rock faults required Jefferson to be moved to Washington's left and pushed Theodore Roosevelt a little into the background.

How many of the more than two million annual visitors to Mount Rushmore realize, as they enjoy this and other nearby attractions, that they are in the middle of the 1.2 million-acre Black Hills National Forest? Here, in an area not quite the size of Delaware, the Hills are unspoiled, untamed, almost primeval. Serenity, solitude, and scenery lure the hiker, climber, or bicyclist. Deer, elk, mountain goats, and an occasional eagle make for fine companions, and one can easily imagine oneself transported back to that idyllic time before the Black Hills gold rush of 1876—the last great gold rush in American history.

GRAND CANYON IN MINIATURE

The geological forces that created the Black Hills also created the wholly different White River Badlands. When the Hills were thrust skyward, some 20 million years ago, the marshy terrain in this area was buried under silt and ash. Because of the large number and rich variety of prehistoric mammals found here, the Badlands are considered the birthplace of vertebrate paleontology, and the South Dakota School of Mines and Technology works closely with the park service in preparing and preserving these 23 to 36 million-year-old remnants of the Oligocene era.

But it isn't all work. The Badlands are yet another of South Dakota's many tourist attractions. Visitors come to admire the stark, otherworldly beauty of this 35-by-90-mile region. They are fascinated by the paleontological finds and amazed at just how different this little corner of the state really is.

Today western South Dakota stands virtually unchallenged as the state's tourism mecca, and as that industry commands an ever more important spot in

the state's economy, so too will the West grow ever more prominent. But there is more to this area than tourism. Mining, especially gold, is big business here; so are lumbering and forestry, ranching, and to a lesser extent, farming. And one of the biggest employers in the area is Ellsworth Air Force Base.

Still, this region remains a living memorial to the past, to the days of gold rushes and land rushes, desperadoes and gunslingers, gamblers and prospectors, settlers and Native Americans—a heritage that western South Dakota will keep alive for the entire state for generations to come.

Nestled at the base of limestone palisades, guarded by ranks of aspen, spruce, and ponderosa pine, the many teeming creeks and streams of the Black Hills beckon intrepid fisherfolk such as this well-geared teenager.

CHAPTER FIVE

THE CENTRAL PLAINS: ACROSS THE WIDE MISSOURI

The Missouri River bisects South Dakota geographically and culturally. "The river," as it is universally known here, is the boundary between cowboy country and farm country. One can feel it—and see it—as one crosses the river at Chamberlain. Attitudes, economies, histories, even the landscape—all are different, albeit intertwined. But of course the river is more than a convenience for pigeonholing West and East Riverites. The central part

of the state is and always has been inextricably linked to the river. Important as a transportation artery since at least the days of Lewis and Clark, the Missouri River today is the centerpiece of another of the state's major attractions, the Great Lakes of South Dakota.

WATER WONDERS

There are four Great Lakes—Lake Oahe, Lake Sharpe, Lake Francis Case, and Lewis and Clark Lake—at intervals along the river from centrally located Pierre, the state capital, to Yankton, the old territorial capital, in the extreme southeast corner of the state.

The greatest of these Great Lakes is Oahe—a Sioux word meaning "foundation" or "a place to stand on"—which extends upstream more than 200 miles into North Dakota. Lake Oahe has a shoreline of more than 2,250 miles—longer than the coast of California.

The amazing thing about these pellucid blue expanses is that they were formed not by tectonic upheaval or Ice Age bulldozing, but rather by human intervention: the damming of the Missouri as part of the Pick-Sloan plan for flood control. These imposing barriers

of earth and concrete and steel not only helped tame the once unruly river, but also are home to some of the mightiest hydroelectric power plants around. Oahe Dam, the second largest rolled-earth dam in the world, also houses seven of the largest generators in the world. Big Bend Dam (Lake Sharpe), Fort Randall Dam (Lake Francis Case), and Gavins Point Dam (Lewis and Clark Lake) also create electric power for the region. Into the bargain they created a mecca for boaters, hunters, campers, hikers, anglers, water sports enthusiasts, and anyone who enjoys the sight of a flock of Canada geese winging above the mirrorlike surface of the water.

AN OUTDOOR PARADISE

Truly, this is an Eden for the outdoor enthusiast. Pick a lake, and a staggering menagerie of wildlife can be found

FACING PAGE: *In 1804 Meriwether Lewis admired the grass-scented rolling hills that greeted him from a bluff overlooking the Missouri River. The town of Chamberlain was later built nearby, but views such as this one across Roam Free Park remain largely unchanged.*

ILLUSTRATION, THIS PAGE: © Hilber Nelson; PHOTO, FACING PAGE: © Grace Davies/Photo Network

nearby: mule deer and the once almost extinct white-tailed deer at Lake Francis Case, or smaller game such as red fox, coyote, raccoon, and beaver; deer and pronged-horn antelope, plus mink, fox, and other smaller game at Lake Oahe. The deer and the antelope play at Lake Sharpe, too, as does the seldom seen black-footed ferret. Lewis and Clark Lake boasts waterfowl and other bird life in abundance: wood ducks, teal, geese, northern bald and golden eagles, and wild turkeys among them, as well as game animals. What about the one that got away? Fishing at any of the Great Lakes may well yield pike, cat-fish, walleye, crappies, bass, and sauger. In 1960 the United States Fish and Wildlife Service opened the Gavins Point National Fish Hatchery, one of 70 federal hatcheries, which to date has produced almost one bil-lion fish for stocking throughout the Midwest. And the

America's greatest bronc buster, Casey Tibbs (1929–1990), of Fort Pierre, won the world saddle bronc riding championship at 19. Here, cowboys at the annual Fort Pierre Rodeo carry on a proud tradition.

Fort Randall Bald Eagle Refuge was one of the first in the nation to be set aside for the protection of that great bird.

COWS AND CASH CROPS

Here in the central portion of the state, livestock—espe-cially dairy cows—is the main agricultural undertaking. But farms still dot the plains, and among them, in the north-central region, you do encounter a very unusual commercial crop: sunflowers. South Dakota is one of only four states that raise sunflowers commercially, and is the second highest producer of the seeds, which are used primarily for sunflower oil. About 25 percent of the sunflowers grown in the United States come from this little pocket in north-central South Dakota.

Of course, more traditional crops have their place here as well. Farther south, oats and sorghum are important, while winter wheat is raised in the warmer central and western regions of the state. Spring wheat does better in the cooler areas of the north-central region. Hay is raised almost everywhere. But again, livestock commands the lion's share of agricultural endeavors in these central regions. In fact, livestock—dairy cattle, beef cattle, hogs, sheep, and lambs—is really the most important component of the state's agricultural economy. Traditionally, South Dakota ranks in the top 10 in U.S. livestock production.

This red fox shares his home on Lake Francis Case with many other species of wildlife, including white-tailed deer, coyote, and beaver.

GOING TO TOWN

Although most of the population of the state is not found here in the Great Lakes region, the political center of the state certainly is. Pierre (pronounced "peer"), the capital of South Dakota, is located almost exactly in the center of the state, which is largely how it came to be the capital in the first place. Besides being the seat of government Pierre is developing a reputation as a center for tourism and cultural events in its own right. The opulent, copper-domed capitol building is one of the nation's finest and well worth visiting. But that isn't all there is to see or do here: The South Dakota Cultural Heritage Center, the South Dakota Discovery Center and Aquarium, the Fort Pierre National Grassland, and Oahe Dam and Lake Oahe are all in the area. Nearby Indian reservations—Standing Rock, Lower Brule, and Crow Creek—provide their own unique cultural offerings.

CHAPTER SIX

THE NORTHEAST: GIFTS OF THE GLACIERS

Before the completion of the Pick-Sloan project, South Dakota was considered a water-poor state. And yet, even before the great dams were erected, the Mount Rushmore State boasted a fair number of natural lakes—more than 120 of them in fact, in the northeast region alone. These icy cold bodies were left behind by the retreating glaciers that formed eastern South Dakota some 20,000 years ago. Some are rather small, no more than a few acres, but others swell to as much as 16,000 acres, and have played a significant role in this region since ancient times.

Two of these lakes, Lake Traverse and Big Stone Lake, lie strung along the Minnesota border, almost touching one another. Yet because of a north-south continental divide, Lake Traverse empties to the north, flowing via the Red River into Hudson Bay, while the outlet waters of Big Stone Lake follow a more traditional course, journeying southward and eventually emptying into the Gulf of Mexico.

Besides water, the glaciers left another going-away present: rock. Lots of it. Quarrying, which has long been big business throughout eastern South Dakota, is especially significant in the northeast, with two major granite quarries of international repute. Much of the stone found here is of a rosy, evenly variegated hue that is unique to this part of the globe. Granite from quarries near the aptly named Big Stone Lake are used in monuments, office buildings, and increasingly, homes across the country and around the world.

ARTS VISUAL AND LITERARY

This portion of the state also stakes a claim in the world of art and literature. L. Frank Baum lived in Aberdeen shortly before writing *The Wonderful Wizard of Oz,* the first of his more than 60 children's books. Terry Redlin, one of the country's favorite wildlife artists, grew up in Watertown, where a few years ago he built his Redlin Art Center, a $10 million gift to the state that once awarded him a $1,500 art scholarship. And De Smet may have been named for a Jesuit missionary who dedicated his life to the local Indians, but it is more famous today as Laura Ingalls Wilder's "Little Town on the Prairie."

HUNTERS' DELIGHT

With so many lakes in this region, it is yet another outdoor playground for hunters, anglers, campers, and

FACING PAGE: *Watertown's Kampeska Heritage Museum showcases pioneer life in this region through artifacts and recreated scenes. The museum building is a former Carnegie library built in 1905.*

ILLUSTRATION, THIS PAGE: © Hilber Nelson; PHOTO, FACING PAGE: © Greg Ryan–Sally Beyer

other lovers of nature. Walleye dominate the lakes of the northeast, but smallmouth and largemouth bass, bullhead, yellow perch, and northern pike all vie for the hook, too. The ring-necked pheasant—South Dakota's state bird and probably most popular game—was first introduced to the area near here, and it has thrived. The area's location along a major migratory flyway means monumental flocks of virtually all kinds of waterfowl. Snow geese in the hundreds of thousands stop over every year at the Sand Lake National Wildlife Refuge near Columbia. South Dakota is one of the nation's top duck producers. And hunters have excellent luck with coyote, fox, the ubiquitous white-tailed deer, and smaller furbearing game.

As the glaciers gouged out this region of the state, they also laid the groundwork for the farmland for which South Dakota is famous. Here in the northeast corn is an important crop—although conditions for

Since Congress's passage of the Indian Gaming Regulatory Act in 1988, Native Americans in South Dakota have been enjoying newfound prosperity. Revenues from gaming halls such as the Dakota Sioux Casino help reservations build houses, roads, schools, and a more secure economic future for their people.

corn growing are better in the southeastern portion of the state. Soybean growing is significant here, too. And there are small pockets of rye, flaxseed, and potato growing in this region as well. Most of the state's dairy cows are concentrated in northeastern South Dakota, with roughly 20 cows per 1,000 acres around Grant and Deuel Counties.

Northeastern South Dakota is also the site of the Royal River Casino at Flandreau, owned and operated by the Flandreau Santee Sioux tribe, which features Las Vegas–style stage shows in addition to poker, blackjack, slot machines, and bingo. Traveling north from

RIGHT: *Under an evening sky, costumed actors re-create scenes from the life and times of Laura Ingalls Wilder. For three weekends every summer the population of De Smet swells from 1,200 to over 8,000 during the Laura Ingalls Wilder Pageant.*

Flandreau you come upon the Sisseton-Wahpeton Indian Reservation, which hosts three popular casinos of its own: Dakota Sioux, north of Watertown; Dakota Connection, near Sisseton; and Dakota Magic, near the North Dakota border. Among them, the three offer various table games, slot machines, bingo, and pari-mutuel offtrack betting. In addition, the reservation itself features the Tekakwitha Fine Arts and Interpretive Center, and the Sisseton-Wahpeton Dakota Oyate host the International Powwow every Independence Day weekend, featuring more than 900 competing dancers from across the United States.

BELOW: *Storybook Land in Aberdeen features the "Land of Oz" among its fairy tale and nursery rhyme themes. The park also offers water activities, hiking and biking trails, camping, and miniature golf.*

CHAPTER SEVEN

THE SOUTHEAST: THE WILD, WILD EAST

Here is the gently rolling prairie farmland that most folks think of when they hear "South Dakota." The south-eastern portion of the state boasts some of the richest, most productive farmland in the world. Statewide, agriculture accounts for some $3 billion in cash receipts per annum. Forty percent of the agricultural economy is given over to crop production, with a goodly portion of that in eastern, especially southeastern, South Dakota.

Actually, this corner of the state is at the very northwest corner of the corn belt, so it is no surprise that corn accounts for just over 50 percent of harvested crops. Most of that goes to feed animals: In the west, cattle are grass-fed, while in the east, they are corn-fed. Corn is also grown here for human consumption, of course, and its use in producing the gasoline additive ethanol is becoming more important to the local economy. Soybean growing is also a significant part of the agriculture in this region. The ever-increasing demand for soy products around the world has resulted in a dramatic rise in production in the state.

Although some cattle production takes place in this region—mainly beef cows—the southeast is better known for hog and pig production, with Yankton County having the greatest concentration per 1,000 acres.

URBAN SPRAWL, SOUTH DAKOTA–STYLE
But it is not all farms, of course, and not all South Dakotans are farmers, even if they find themselves only a step or two removed from the land. Here in southeastern South Dakota is Sioux Falls, which has overcome its rather quaint name to become a thriving regional center for finance, health care, retailing, and the arts. This city was recently ranked by *Money* magazine as the best place to live in America. Having passed the 100,000 population mark—nearer to 120,000 when you factor in the market region—Sioux Falls is in some ways the *de facto* capital of South Dakota. Its cornerstone shopping complex, The Empire/Empire East, gets more visitors each year than Mount Rushmore. Its two general hospitals, constantly expanding, are increasingly seen as offering medical services on a par with the best of Minneapolis, Rochester, or Denver. Two liberal-arts colleges, several community colleges, postsecondary technical and business schools, and a local satellite of the state

FACING PAGE: *"The World's Only Corn Palace," in Mitchell, sees more than three-quarters of a million visitors every year. The building's exterior art is changed every summer, but the murals inside are permanent, with six exceptional panels designed by Yanktonai Sioux painter and former state artist laureate Oscar Howe.*

ILLUSTRATION, THIS PAGE: © Hilber Nelson; PHOTO, FACING PAGE: © South Dakota Tourism

university system make this a center for education and research. Numerous museums, galleries, and theaters—and the recently opened Washington Pavilion of Arts and Science, with its 1,900-seat Great Hall in the Performing Arts Center—make this a cultural haven. The presence of the EROS (Earth Resources Observation Systems) Data Center in nearby Garretson links Sioux Falls to the stars. And, of course, everyone with one of those Holstein-motif boxes in the attic knows that Gateway Computers is headquartered here, in North Sioux City to be exact.

Southeastern South Dakota also features the leafy, vaguely European-flavored city of Yankton, once the capital of Dakota Territory, today a picturesque gem on the Missouri River, home to Lewis and Clark Lake. That lake and its surrounding resorts, campgrounds, and marinas may be Yankton's biggest draw today, but history buffs come to visit the Dakota Territorial Museum, which includes an exact replica of the original territorial capitol.

One of the flagship campuses in the state university system is found in this region as well, in Vermillion: the University of South Dakota, headquarters for the state's law and medical schools.

Sioux Falls' 62 public green spaces include Falls Park, where the city's watery namesake can be seen tumbling along its age-old path. Residents also enjoy the area's cultural offerings, low crime rate, affordable housing, plentiful jobs, and relaxed lifestyle.

BAD OLD DAYS

So southeastern South Dakota is and always has been calm, placid, and bucolic, yes? Well, no; the past here is a little checkered in places, and even the farmlands have a Wild West connection. They say that Jesse James once eluded a posse by jumping Devil's Gulch, a 20-foot-wide chasm near Garretson. Of course, his horse did most of the work, and you can get across by footbridge today. More recently, in 1934, members of the infamous Dillinger gang robbed a bank in downtown Sioux Falls and escaped with $46,000 in loot. It is doubtful that Dillinger himself was involved, but eyewitnesses insisted that Dillinger's crony George "Baby Face" Nelson was among the group, and the robbery fit Dillinger's *modus operandi*. The crooks lost their pursuers in the unpaved back roads of farmland near what is today The Empire/Empire East shopping mall.

PHOTO: © Eric R. Berndt/Midwestock

FUN AND GAMES

Outdoor activities are king in this corner of the state. Lewis and Clark Lake alone offers camping, boating, fishing, and more. Hunters, anglers, and campers have additional favorite spots throughout the region.

The southeast is home to the state's burgeoning professional sports scene, represented by the Sioux Falls Canaries in baseball, the Sioux Falls Skyforce in basketball, and the start-up Sioux Falls Stampede in hockey. It should be pointed out that, out west, the Rapid City Thrillers is a powerhouse basketball team, too. Professional and semi-pro football have had a rougher go of it here, perhaps because East River folk tend to be firm fans of the Minnesota Vikings while West Riverites lean toward the Denver Broncos. But the region and the state are on the grow, and there is no reason to think that the new millennium will lack pro football on the local South Dakota sports menu.

THE BEST OF BOTH WORLDS

It is no overstatement to say that most of South Dakota's growth in recent decades, and for the foreseeable future, is in the southeastern region. This is true not only of population—after a decline in the first half of this century, South Dakota has enjoyed a small but steady increase in the last decades—but also of business and industry, since Sioux Falls and environs are already well established as a center of finance, health care, transportation, and technology.

But even as the state becomes increasingly modern and "high tech,"

South Dakotans are acutely aware of—and appreciative of—their roots, and take great pains to preserve them. It seems safe to bet that South Dakotans, in the upcoming 100 years, will continue to simultaneously embrace the future while honoring the heritage and traditions of the early years. In that model, the four regions of the Mount Rushmore state will continue their unique dovetailing well into the new millennium.

The southeast's rich soil contributes to the state's $1.2 billion annual crop harvest. These wheat fields near Salem are a typical sight little more than a stone's throw from metropolitan Sioux Falls. South Dakota is among the top 10 wheat-producing states.

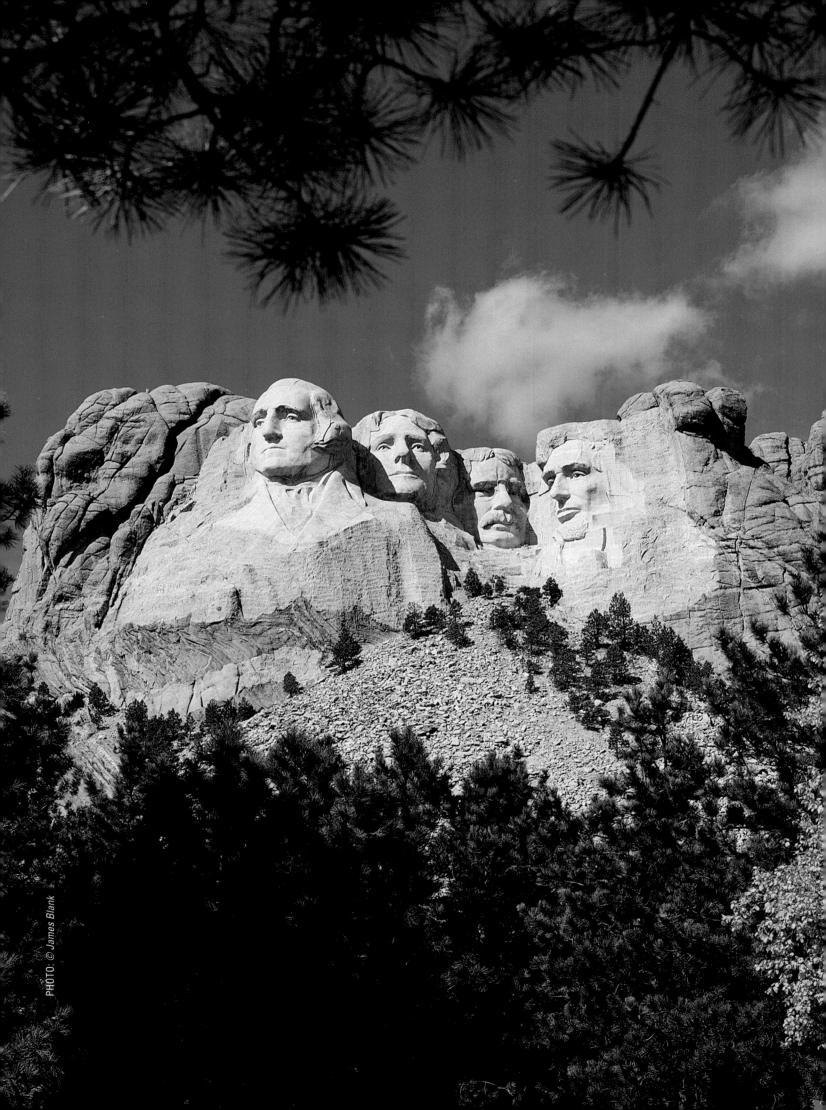

PART THREE

SPIRIT OF SUCCESS

At the beginning of the twentieth century South Dakota was an agricultural state, dependent upon the farmer for economic survival. It is still closely tied to the land; yet the state's economy has changed radically. Tourism is the number two industry, and other strong economic forces have emerged: Since the 1970s, South Dakota has been a player in the field of high finance, and when Citibank moved its credit card processing center here in 1980, it opened the floodgates for other financial enterprises. Meanwhile, Sioux Falls' two major hospitals began to make that city a regional health care center, an effort that continues today. High technology has had a niche here since the 1960s, but the arrival of computer powerhouse Gateway in 1990 added fame to fortune. South Dakota has one of the "most wired" colleges in the nation, a fully networked school system, a statewide video communications network, and more miles of fiber-optic cable than any other state. And more than 500 companies relocated or expanded here in 1998 alone.

What accounts for all this growth? Many things, to be sure. A central location, enhanced by two major interstate highways. A favorable business climate with no corporate income tax, business inventory tax, personal property tax, or personal income tax. Clean air, clean water, little crime. The world-famous midwestern work ethic, and the equally famous friendliness of the plains dwellers.

Small wonder that recent years have seen South Dakota rise to the top 10 of *Site Selection*'s "most livable" states. In fact, it's no wonder at all.

Looking to the future as well as the past, the faces on Mount Rushmore represent four milestones in U.S. history: birth (Washington), growth (Jefferson), preservation (Lincoln), and development (Roosevelt).

CHAPTER EIGHT

THE HIGH-TECH VANGUARD

If you are entertaining a covered-wagon-and-sod-house image of the Mount Rushmore State, now would be a good time to update it. South Dakota is no stranger to high technology, nor is the state a Johnny-come-lately to the high-tech bandwagon. Take Daktronics, Inc. This manufacturer of electronic scoreboards and computer-programmable displays has been in business in Brookings since 1968. Founded by two South Dakota State

University electrical engineering professors, Daktronics joined the big leagues when it landed the contract to provide electronic scoreboards for the 1980 Winter Olympic Games in Lake Placid. Today more than 50 countries utilize the company's displays for sporting events, time-and-temperature signs, departure and arrival information, and legislative voting systems.

Another veteran South Dakota high-tech actor is Sencore, a 47-year-old firm headquartered in Sioux Falls since 1971. The company is a world-renowned manufacturer of electronic test instruments for the service and repair of televisions, VCRs, computer monitors, camcorders, and other electronic gizmos.

LodgeNet Entertainment Corporation began supplying satellite TV services to hotels and motels in 1980. Now it provides video-on-demand products, including movies and Super Nintendo video games, to nearly 700,000 guest rooms across the country.

Instances of South Dakota's emerging importance in the world of high technology are everywhere. Hutchinson Technology Incorporated, which makes about 70 percent of the world's suspension assemblies for disk drives, moved its assembly operation to Sioux Falls in 1988, and now is the city's sixth largest employer. Cabletron Systems

of New Hampshire, a designer of computer network and software products, expanded to South Dakota in 1998, creating 135 high-tech jobs in the bargain.

THOSE SPOTTED BOXES

South Dakota's most famous high-tech brand has to be Gateway, Inc., an internationally known personal computers company. Begun in an Iowa farmhouse in 1985, Gateway today boasts revenues in excess of $6 billion and employs more than 19,000 people around the world. In South Dakota, where the company maintains one of its headquarters (others are in California and New York), Gateway employs more than 7,000 people. It is Sioux Falls' seventh largest employer. Nowadays, when you mention you're from South Dakota, you often hear, "Hey, I have one of your computers!"

NUMBER, PUH-LEEZ

Even in a large, sparsely populated state such as South Dakota, we take telephone service for granted. The

In addition to bringing programming to guest rooms across North America, LodgeNet Entertainment now licenses its technology to firms in Japan, South Korea, Brazil, Panama, Venezuela, and Peru.

PHOTO: © Stuart Melby/Courtesy, Daktronics

technology came to the larger communities first: Sioux Falls had phone service as early as 1882. The more remote areas had to be patient as wires were stretched across the landscape. But by the 1960s phone service was available to virtually all of South Dakota.

For most of this history, the main player was U S WEST Communications, formerly known as Northwestern Bell. U S WEST still supplies dial tone to most South Dakotans' phones, as well as an ever-growing smorgasbord of services that phone customers have come to expect from their providers: intrastate long distance, Internet service, voice mail, and more.

Other players in South Dakota include numerous smaller independent, municipal, and cooperative telephone companies. Naturally, the major national long-distance suppliers all have footholds in South Dakota: AT&T, MCI, Sprint, and others.

Cellular technology came to the state fairly early on, too, in the late 1980s. Some local companies, such as Midco Communications, climbed aboard the bandwagon early. Other regional and national companies were quick to join them—companies such as CommNet and

Daktronics, Inc., started out designing and manufacturing electronic voting systems for state legislatures. Today Daktronics has the most complete line of electronic displays in the world.

Cellular One—the result being that scarcely a corner of the state is out of cellular reach as the new millennium hurtles toward us.

PHONING THE FUTURE

But the Mount Rushmore State is not sitting back waiting for the telephone to ring. It is closing the twentieth century with a typically proactive approach to technology. The state has enacted legislation to support telecommunications infrastructure for business and industry, and to ensure that the technology reaches even the smallest communities. A joint venture between the state and smaller government entities to share telecommunications services has resulted in monthly rate drops of as much as 52 percent for some cities, counties, and schools, with long-distance savings of up to 66 percent. The state has established and is continuously expanding its Rural Development Telecommunications Network

(RDTN), a statewide video communications network. No wonder Governor William Janklow is fond of pointing out that South Dakota has more miles of fiber-optic cable than any other state.

again stepped up to the plate early on. Today South Dakota is thoroughly on-line. The state has had an informative Web site for some years now; every department, agency, or bureau also has a home page. State universities make extensive use of the Internet, offering graduate and undergraduate courses via the Internet to students across South Dakota and around the world.

As the twentieth century draws to a close, the Internet is still pretty friendly toward mom-and-pop service providers, at least in South Dakota. There are dozens of dial-up access providers around the state, in dozens of different sizes, such as Black Hills Online in Spearfish, ICONtrol in Watertown, DakotaConnect in

LET'S GO SURFIN' NOW

South Dakota routinely finds itself on various "most wired" lists. In 1999 six of the state's high schools landed among *FamilyPC* magazine's "Top 100 Most Wired High Schools"; and Dakota State University checked in at tenth on *Yahoo! Internet Life* magazine's "America's 100 Most Wired Colleges," up from twelfth in 1998—and the Madison institution wasn't even on the list in 1997! Also, South Dakota is just about finished wiring all 176 school districts for the "information superhighway."

Surprised? You shouldn't be. The Internet was custom-made for a large, spread-out state, and South Dakota once

The Earth Resources Observation Systems (EROS) Data Center, near Sioux Falls, distributes U.S. government–owned, nonmilitary satellite images and aerial photography to scientists worldwide.

Pierre, and Splitrock Internet in Garretson among the small- to midsized ones; plus a number of cooperative or utility-company services such as Sully Buttes Telephone Co-Op in Highmore; and even one or two folks still running "modem shops" in their basements, mostly for the fun of it.

Increasingly, bigger players are carving out niches in the market—Dakota Telecommunications Group (DTG), RapidNet, and Cybernex notable among them. In addition, cable television companies have begun offering "cable modems" to subscribers in the larger communities. Sioux Falls Cable began the service in the late 1990s. Others, such as TCI Cablevision in Rapid City, are readying to provide the linkup early in 2000. Colleges, universities, and some businesses are linked directly to the "backbone" of the Internet, usually via the Earth Resources Observation Systems (EROS) Data Center at Garretson.

LOOKING UP

EROS represents another example of South Dakota's early affinity for high technology. The data center opened in 1971 with the mission to receive, process, and distribute data from NASA's *Landsat* satellites. Today EROS is the repository for the world's largest collection of earth images acquired from space or from aircraft—10.2 million frames of photographic data and more than 152,000

U S WEST's $400 million investment in South Dakota includes two synchronous optical network (SONET) rings to ensure uninterrupted transmissions. Pictured is the company's Sioux Falls headquarters.

digital tapes. And all of it is sitting smack-dab in the middle of southeastern South Dakota farm country.

OPEN ROAD AHEAD

So you see, South Dakotans have loved high tech since long before it was fashionable. That is not going to change in the new millennium—except perhaps that the Mount Rushmore State will be even farther ahead of the pack.

PICTURE THIS

In January of 1999 South Dakota's Rural Development Telecommunications Network (RDTN) activated a video bridge that allows for out-of-network videoconferencing, allowing participants with different equipment, working at different data rates, to conference. In addition, RDTN's Continuous Presence enables participants at each site to view up to four other sites simultaneously.

DAKTRONICS, INC.

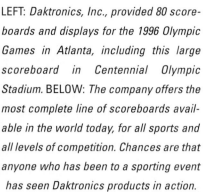

LEFT: Daktronics, Inc., provided 80 scoreboards and displays for the 1996 Olympic Games in Atlanta, including this large scoreboard in Centennial Olympic Stadium. BELOW: The company offers the most complete line of scoreboards available in the world today, for all sports and all levels of competition. Chances are that anyone who has been to a sporting event has seen Daktronics products in action.

Daktronics equipment is keeping score, informing, and entertaining people throughout the world. A recognized leader in electronic displays, Daktronics offers world-class technology in scoreboards, programmable displays, and large-screen video systems. The company has grown because of its ability to provide innovative communication solutions for a wide variety of clients.

Founded in 1968 by two professors of electrical engineering at South Dakota State University in Brookings, the company designed and manufactured an electronic voting system for the Utah House of Representatives. That first major project launched a product line. Since then Daktronics has developed electronic voting systems for a majority of state legislatures and a complete line of scoreboards for virtually all sports and all levels of competition. It offers computer-programmable displays in incandescent lamp, LED (light-emitting diode), and reflective technologies.

In the early 1970s Daktronics ventured into electronic scoreboards with the Matside® wrestling scoreboard, which enabled fans, referees, and competitors to see times and scores without missing any of the action. The development of this unique product led Daktronics to develop the All Sport® line, one of the most complete lines of scoreboards available today.

Daktronics offers displays based on such technologies as incandescent lamp, LED (light-emitting diode), and reflection to help businesses promote their products and services.

More than 1,000 colleges and universities across the United States use Daktronics scoreboards and displays. In addition, Daktronics systems are used by many professional teams and facilities for NBA, NFL, NHL, and Major League Baseball games. A few of the notable venues using Daktronics systems are the Great Western Forum, home of the Los Angeles Lakers; Raymond James Stadium, home of the Tampa Bay Buccaneers; the Continental Airlines Arena at the Meadowlands Sports Complex, home of the New Jersey Devils; and SAFECO Field, home of the Seattle Mariners. Daktronics also has developed transportable systems for clients, such as the Professional Golf Association for the PGA Tour and Senior PGA Tour.

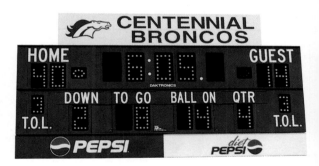

KEEPING THE SCORE

The level of popularity in the United States of Daktronics scoreboards and displays also is seen in other countries. In 1978 Daktronics was awarded a major contract to provide nine scoreboards for the 1980 Olympic Winter Games in Lake Placid. The project gave the company an opportunity to show its capabilities to the world during this high-profile, high-pressure international event. The project

turned out to be a major success for Daktronics. Contracts for other important international events followed, including World Cup events, the Pan American Games, the Commonwealth Games, the All-Africa Games, and additional Olympic Games. Daktronics will supply the majority of scoreboards and displays for the 2000 Summer Olympic Games in Sydney, Australia. Daktronics products inform and entertain millions of people each day in more than 60 different countries.

The company also is a leader in the design and manufacture of scoreboards for smaller sports facilities, for customers such as schools and departments of parks and recreation. Daktronics Scoreboard Sales & Service® organization, with a growing number of offices around the United States, provides technical and installation service and support for scoreboard and display customers nationwide.

The first computer-programmable displays developed by Daktronics were digital displays of temperature readings and time of day. Today Daktronics offers one of the world's most complete lines of information display systems so that customers can choose the best technology available for their particular application and situation. Information displays by Daktronics now are used by banks, shopping centers, auto dealerships, gas stations, hotels and motels, casinos, and retail stores as well as for sports teams and facilities. Display technologies include DataTrac™, InfoNet™, and Galaxy™ LED–based systems; SunSpot® and Starburst® incandescent displays; Glow Cube® and MagneView™ reflective displays; ProStar™ VideoPlus displays; and Venus® control systems.

Another important part of its business is providing display systems that assist travelers. Daktronics displays are located on major roadways, at train and subway terminals, and in airports to help travelers reach their destinations safely and on time.

ProStar™ VideoPlus displays were introduced by Daktronics in 1997. This large-screen video technology uses red, green, and blue LEDs to show live action and instant replays in 16.7 million vibrant colors. The development of this technology has enabled Daktronics to provide truly integrated scoring and video systems at major sports venues. ProStar™ technology is available in many different pixel sizes and display configurations.

As the company has grown and increased its customer base worldwide, modular design, quality control, and manufacturing integrity have taken on added importance. To remain focused on high-quality products that are delivered on time and to provide the solutions its customers need and expect, Daktronics is a vertically integrated company with world-class engineering and manufacturing capabilities. The sales organization is market oriented in order to better understand the needs of customers and deliver products that meet those needs.

DAKTRONICS, INC.

"Daktronics is a growing and exciting company in a growing and exciting industry," says Dr. Al Kurtenbach, company president and cofounder. "Our past success and continued growth are based on developing communication solutions for our customers. We've become a leader in this industry thanks to hard-working employees who design, market, and manufacture the best display products in the world."

Daktronics products help travelers reach their destinations safely and on time. The company's displays are located over highways, in bus and train terminals, and in airports throughout the United States.

HUTCHINSON TECHNOLOGY INCORPORATED

HUTCHINSON

TECHNOLOGY

INCORPORATED

IS A WORLDWIDE

LEADER IN THE

DESIGN AND

MANUFACTURE OF

SUSPENSION

ASSEMBLIES FOR

DISK DRIVES OF

ALL SIZES FOR

USE IN PERSONAL

AND BUSINESS

COMPUTER SYSTEMS

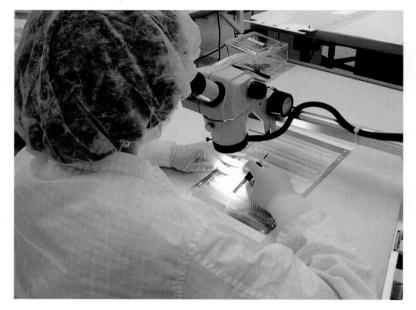

A quality assurance auditor at Hutchinson Technology Inc. uses a scope to inspect trace panels prior to the suspension assembly manufacturing process.

With worldwide sales of both personal and business computers growing exponentially in recent years, a significant computer component from Hutchinson Technology Incorporated has captured nearly two-thirds of its domestic and international market.

Hutchinson Technology produces suspension assemblies for all sizes of disk drives made by the major disk drive manufacturers supplying the computer market. The suspension assembly is the precise metal spring that holds the drive's read/ write head at a microscopic distance above the disk. High-precision suspensions are critical to the operation of the drive.

The company was established in 1965 in Hutchinson, Minnesota, as Hutchinson Industrial Corporation. Its founders, two young entrepreneurs, envisioned a line of products for rocket guidance systems. Later the corporate name was changed to Hutchinson Technology Incorporated to better reflect the company's emerging high-tech business.

Like most companies, Hutchinson Technology started out small and severely undercapitalized. With only $30,000 in funding, the budget was so tight that the entire company was initially housed in a chicken coop. In fact the renovated structure achieved the distinction of being the only NASA-certified chicken coop in the country. It is still in use today on the site in Hutchinson where corporate headquarters is located. From these roots, the company has matured into an industry leader with manufacturing plants in Eau Claire, Wisconsin; Plymouth, Minnesota; and Sioux Falls, South Dakota, as well as international sales and service support operations in Japan, China, Singapore, and the Netherlands.

Hutchinson Technology continues to grow. Its Sioux Falls manufacturing operation, started in 1988, was expanded in 1998 with the completion of a new 299,000-square-foot plant. The company now employs more than 8,100 people at facility locations worldwide.

In the past several years Hutchinson Technology has benefited from two trends: first, the increasing sales of computer systems, and second, the increasing importance of the suspension assembly in permitting improved disk drive performance—which produces greater data storage capacity, allows faster access to data, improves reliability, and lowers costs. The company fills an important niche in a constantly growing market.

Hutchinson Technology has achieved and maintains leadership by developing upgraded suspensions in anticipation of market needs and by continually improving its proprietary manufacturing processes and equipment.

With disk drive sales expected to continue growing at a brisk pace for at least the next decade, Hutchinson Technology is dedicated to aiding that growth with innovative new products.

The company produces TSA Suspensions, which incorporate electrical leads that connect directly with the read/write head and transmit data to the control circuits of the disk drive. The integral copper traces have leads pre-positioned on one end to match bonding pads on the flying head and on the other end to match the drive's pre-amp chip. This allows for automated bonding, instead of the manual bonding required with individual wires. For Hutchinson Technology's customers, TSA Suspensions minimize handling damage, simplify the electrical termination process, and lower capital investment and assembly costs.

By employing conductor geometries selected for high-speed signal transmission, TSA suspensions offer electrical properties superior to those of fine twisted wires. Unlike wires, the integral conductors in TSA suspensions are not subject to inadvertent bending at the time

Hutchinson Technology employees work with automation and other advanced technologies to create the company's high-precision disk drive suspension assemblies that successfully compete on a global scale.

the head is attached, nor are they as susceptible to bending when subjected to the mechanical shock encountered when a laptop computer is dropped or otherwise jarred. The disk drive industry is expected to continue to grow as new applications for disk drive storage emerge, such as digital VCRs, digital cameras, Internet services, voice messaging, and increased computer graphic capabilities. Disk drive manufacture will be at least as technically challenging and competitive in the future as it has been in the past.

To keep up with accelerating demand and technical changes, Hutchinson Technology continues to invest in increased production capacity as well as specialized equipment and advanced processes, much of which is designed, constructed, and perfected by the company's own employees. As the information age unfolds, extraordinary skills and capabilities such as those of Hutchinson Technology promise to command greater and greater value in the disk drive market as well as other markets where reliable, high-precision components and products are essential.

HUTCHINSON TECHNOLOGY'S VISION
Passionately enabling the information age

This Sioux Falls plant is the South Dakota manufacturing facility of Hutchinson Technology, headquartered in Hutchinson, Minnesota. Here and at its other plants, both domestic and international, the company produces its computer disk drive suspension assemblies and supplies nearly 60 percent of all suspensions sold into disk drives.

CHAPTER NINE

SOUTH DAKOTA MADE

In the Mount Rushmore State, technology goes hand in glove with manufacturing. Many, if not most, of our high-tech companies are themselves manufacturers: Gateway, Hutchinson Technology Incorporated, Sencore, and Daktronics, Inc., among them. But the list is much longer and broader than that. After all, manufacturing employs nearly 50,000 South Dakotans, and generates more than $3 billion a year in gross sales.

LAYING IT ON THE TABLE

As you might expect, much of that action is in the food processing sector, which employs more than 7,500 workers. Food processing covers everything from meat packing and processing to dairy operations to the manufacture of snack foods such as the Dakota Style line of potato chips, which are taken from field to supermarket by the family-owned Campbell Farms at Clark in northeastern South Dakota. The major soft drink companies are well represented here, too. Pepsi-Cola has operations in Mobridge, Huron, Mitchell, Aberdeen, Pierre, and a new bottling facility at Sioux Falls; Coca-Cola is similarly entrenched.

THINGS THAT BUZZ, BEEP, AND GO

Perhaps surprising, though, the lion's share of the state's manufacturing activity is in the machinery and equipment sector, which provides almost 15,000 jobs. Knowing that, it should come as no surprise at all that the manufacturing sector to add the most jobs is machinery and equipment. Once again, the Mount Rushmore State's high-tech pedigree points the way to the future. That category added more than 400 jobs

between 1997 and 1998 alone—and has played a key role in increasing South Dakota's gross sales from less than $2 billion at the beginning of the 1990s to more than $3 billion as that decade closes.

THE WORLD STAGE

In addition to firms such as Daktronics and Gateway, South Dakota is home to several other world-renowned manufacturers. Take Aerostar International, a wholly owned subsidiary of South Dakota's Raven Industries. If you have ever watched a hot-air balloon waft across the sky, or laughed as an inflated cartoon character floated above a Thanksgiving or New Year's Day parade, then you have probably seen an Aerostar/Raven product. Besides being preeminent in the world of hot- and cold-air and helium inflatables, Raven's nationwide divisions also manufacture plastics, electronics, and sewn products—everything from pickup truck toppers to ultrathin and reinforced plastic films, from industrial controls to ultrasonic soil-depth control

The fastest growing retail businesses are eating and drinking establishments, such as these in Sioux Falls' Empire/Empire East food court. The retail trade in South Dakota employs nearly 70,000 people.

devices, from severe-weather uniforms for police and government agencies to sportswear.

Another South Dakota–based company with a national presence is Brookings' Larson Manufacturing, maker of storm doors and windows. In fact, Larson is the

United Defense's Armament Systems Division plant in Aberdeen supplies equipment to the U.S. Navy and allies worldwide. The nationally recognized management style at Aberdeen fosters employee involvement and a participatory management style.

largest storm door manufacturer in the industry, specializing in wood-core storm doors, which it created, as well as more than a half dozen other styles. Founded in 1956, Larson today employs more than 1,200 people across the country, just over half of them in Brookings.

Also in Brookings, another actor on the world stage, the far-flung 3M Corporation, manufactures surgical adhesives used in hospitals and clinics throughout the United States. That isn't 3M's only presence in South Dakota. A 3M division in Aberdeen makes various other medical supplies and, like its companion in Brookings, is one of the town's major employers. Call it reciprocity: Back in 1907 South Dakotan William McKnight saved the struggling Minnesota company from ruin and later built it into the Fortune 500 giant we know today.

The giant Toshiba company is at home in many corners of the world, including Mitchell, where it makes

CHANGING GEARS

Thomas Fawick was 19 years old in 1908. That was the year he test-drove his first automobile through the streets of an awestruck Sioux Falls. Two years later he introduced a Fawick Flyer with four doors—the first such car in America. A childhood friend bought the car, and former President Theodore Roosevelt rode in it when he visited the town. In all, Thomas Fawick built five Fawick Flyers and sold them for $3,000 each before leaving Sioux Falls and the auto business. He went on to design the Airflex clutch, which was used in thousands of U.S. Navy vessels in World War II and is still manufactured today.

toner products. Mitchell may well be the toner capital of South Dakota: Mitchell Plastics manufactures the cartridges that hold the messy but essential powder.

SOUTH DAKOTA WIRED—WITH A TWIST

Have you ever used a plastic-coated wire tie closure, also known as a "twist tie"? Odds are pretty good it was made in Sioux Falls by Bedford Industries, a leader in not only regular twist ties but also Bedford Bendable Ribbon, a wired ribbon used in crafts and floral applications. Bedford is the leading wired ribbon producer in the United States, although its products are sold worldwide. Bedford also is active in manufacturing and marketing "lumber" made of recycled plastics through its Bedford Technology division.

SALES ARE UP

Retail and wholesale operations are another important and growing component of the South Dakota economy. The wholesale trade employs around 20,000 South Dakotans; the retail trade closer to 70,000. The state's two major retailing centers are Rushmore Mall in Rapid City and The Empire/Empire East in Sioux Falls, but hundreds of retailers great and small throughout the state, as well as downtown districts in several cities, have begun to re-emerge as retailing centers.

The wholesale trade here runs the gamut from food products—predominantly meat packers and statewide dairy wholesalers such as Lakeside, Land O'Lakes, and Wells' Blue Bunny—to Heart of the Earth Handcrafted

The "founder of the modern hot-air balloon," Sioux Falls–based Raven Industries supplies parades and festivals worldwide through its subsidiary Aerostar International. Here, participants at Mitchell's annual Corn Palace Balloon Rally launch an Aerostar product. Along with branch plants and sewing plants scattered across South Dakota, Raven Industries also has plants and distribution centers in Minnesota, Arizona, Alabama, Texas, Ohio, and Missouri.

Soaps to Black Hills Flavored Honey. Increasingly, both retailers and wholesalers are utilizing the worldwide power of the Internet to increase their visibility. Take, for example, Gurney's Seed and Nursery Company, in Yankton, a 130-year-old producer of flower and vegetable seeds and plants. Gurney's sells throughout the continental United States via a catalog its founder started in 1906. Nowadays, you can place an order at Gurney's Web site as well. Even in South Dakota's most traditional industries, high-tech is never far away.

AN EMBARRASSMENT OF RICHES

There are many other companies, great and small, in an amazing variety of enterprises. Electronic Systems, Inc., in Sioux Falls, is a contract electronics manufacturing company, specializing in printed circuit board assemblies and other electronic systems. Sioux Corporation in Beresford makes water heaters for concrete applications, and, through its Sioux Steam Cleaner Corporation, is a leading manufacturer of industrial pressure washers and steam cleaners.

Back on the high-tech side, SCI, Inc., makes computer circuit boards in Rapid City; O.E.M. Worldwide in Spearfish manufactures electronic components; and Midcom Manufacturing in Watertown makes telecommunications transformers. Tendaire/Electrol, based in Beresford, manufactures a wide array of products, from generators to flood lights to control and monitor boxes, for utility companies, municipalities, and highway departments across the United States and around the globe.

All this barely scratches the surface. South Dakota is a light-industry, high-tech cornucopia. South Dakotans love of high technology, great business climate, and fantastic work ethic puts them at the front ranks of manufacturers and distributers in the country and in the world.

PHOTO, FACING PAGE: © Brian Lee/GeoIMAGERY

PEPSI-COLA

With several facilities across the state, Pepsi-Cola is a major factor in South Dakota's growth and economy. Founded in 1898, the parent company recently celebrated its centennial year. One of its commitments was to assure that Pepsi in South Dakota would be an industry leader for the next 100 years.

Pepsi in South Dakota has facilities in Aberdeen, Chamberlain, Huron, Mitchell, Mobridge, Pierre, Rapid City, Sioux Falls, and Watertown. Functions at these locations include manufacturing and bottling, warehousing, distribution, transportation, sales, full-service vending, fountain, and fully staffed service departments. The company's strong brand group

Pepsi Cola's beverage business was founded at the turn of the century by Caleb Bradham, a North Carolina druggist who first formulated Pepsi-Cola in 1898. Today consumers spend about $28 billion on Pepsi-Cola beverages. Brand Pepsi and other Pepsi-Cola products—including Diet Pepsi, Mountain Dew, Diet Mountain Dew, and Pepsi One—account for nearly one-third of total soft drink sales in the United States, a consumer market totaling about $54 billion. © Gene's Studio

includes 84 brands in 14 different packages of soft drinks, juices, and waters.

Many of Pepsi's South Dakota facilities include employees that have more than 20 years of experience with the company. Beyond employment longevity with Pepsi, each worker is committed to providing the best products and service across the state.

Pepsi-Cola's state-of-the-art facilities, such as this Distribution Center at 2400 East 52nd Street North in Sioux Falls, provide excellent service.

BEST PEPSI BOTTLER NATIONWIDE

As one of South Dakota's major companies, Pepsi provides strong support to economic development, the state's tax base, and business purchasing. Pepsi reinvests in equipment, manufacturing facilities, transportation, and services to maintain South Dakota Pepsi's status as the best Pepsi bottlers nationwide. South Dakota bottling operations consistently produce the highest-quality beverages, meeting Pepsi's stringent standards. Over the years, South Dakota Pepsi facilities have been recognized by the Pepsi-Cola Company as the top bottlers nationally for high quality in manufacturing and bottling processes. Translation: Pepsi delivers on service, product, and value.

Because of its distinctive combination of urban and rural communities, the state presents unique challenges. Pepsi uses state-of-the-art delivery systems and customer service procedures to ensure that its customers are supported, regardless of location or needs.

Pepsi-Cola delivery operations are designed to ensure high-quality service regardless of a customer's location or needs. © Gene's Studio

COMMUNITY PARTNERS

The company and its employees are community partners. In local communities across the state, organizations call on Pepsi because of its outstanding commitment to South Dakota. At fairs, concerts, entertainment activities and arts, educational, and sports programs for youths and adults, the company and its employees unobtrusively provide their strength and support, demonstrating every day that South Dakota is a great place to live, work, and do business. Pepsi employees, many of whom are active volunteers in their communities, exemplify great leadership for the company, their communities, and the state of South Dakota.

Pepsi takes great pride in doing business with South Dakota's leading employers. Businesses seeking suppliers for soft drinks, waters, juices, and vending machines choose Pepsi because of the company's full line of service and equipment, its vast array of products, and the commitment of its employees to customer service. The state's businesses know that Pepsi will provide them with across-the-board products, service, and support.

For additional information, contact Pepsi-Cola in Sioux Falls: telephone (800) 873-2652; in Aberdeen: telephone (800) 477-2652; or in Watertown: telephone (800) 944-2652.

Pepsi-Cola showcases its vast array of beverages in some of the industry's most innovative and functional vending machines. © Gene's Studio

CCL LABEL, INC.

CCL LABEL, INC.,

DESIGNS AND

PRODUCES LABELS

OF ALL KINDS,

INCLUDING

PRESSURE-SENSITIVE,

EXPANDED-CONTENT,

AND SPECIALTY

LABELS, FOR

COMPANIES AROUND

THE WORLD

Located in Sioux Falls, South Dakota, CCL Label, Inc., is one of the world's largest label printing facilities, with an employee base of more than 400. CCL is a division of CCL Industries, which is North America's largest producer of pressure-sensitive labels and associated specialty products.

CCL Label manufactures products for such major corporations as Procter & Gamble, Pfizer, G. D. Searle, U.S. Tobacco, Armstrong World Industries, Bristol-Myers Squibb, Armour Swift-Eckrich, American Cyanamid and Oral-B Laboratories, as well as for regional accounts such as John Morrell & Co., Orion Industries, Toshiba, Larson Manufacturing, and Gateway.

Founded in 1946 as Modern Press, the business became a leader in commercial printing. Modern Press–Modern Label was formulated with the introduction of advanced equipment and concepts for printing labels. A new facility was completed in 1959. Additional equipment, business growth, and technology advancement allowed Modern Press to continue to grow.

In 1982 Modern Press was purchased by CCL Industries of Toronto, Canada, and the name was changed to CCL Label in 1990. By the end of that year more than 180 workers were employed. New technologies in label

CCL Label, Inc., headquarters, at 1209 West Bailey in Sioux Falls, is a 200,000-square-foot facility.

manufacturing, production, and printing allowed the company to expand to its present scope and national customer base.

Today CCL Label handles the broad range of label construction design, printing, production, packaging, and support for international customers. With continuing advancements in production techniques, CCL Label operations have gained in cost-effectiveness and the company is increasingly competitive in global markets.

In addition to conventional printing, CCL Label specializes in expanded-content labels, encapsulated coupons, Spin-Formation™ label packaging, patterned adhesive labels, tattoos, in-mold labels, dry-peel coupons, and game pieces, as well as other specialty products designed for specific customers.

At CCL Label, in-house design, prepress planning, and product development capabilities ensure customers a complete cycle of service, from creative concept through final production. The company has invested $20 million in the past three years in printing equipment and facilities. One result of this capital investment is heightened market penetration. CCL Label has seen a 50 percent increase in business volume in less than five years—a significant growth rate for this leading South Dakota firm.

Commercial labels are produced in one of the divisions within the CCL Label Sioux Falls facility.

LAND O'LAKES, INC.

MORE THAN JUST

A BUTTER MAKER,

THE FARMER-OWNED

COOPERATIVE

LAND O'LAKES, INC.

STRIVES TO BE ONE

OF THE BEST FOOD

AND AGRICULTURAL

COMPANIES

IN THE WORLD

Known to millions of consumers across the United States as one of the nation's premier butter makers, Land O'Lakes is more than just a butter company. It is a farmer-owned cooperative with nearly 80 years worth of experience on the farm and in the market.

Land O'Lakes enjoys a strong presence in South Dakota, both in dairy foods and in agricultural services. Headquartered in Sioux Falls, Land O'Lakes runs the largest fluid dairy operation in the state. The company's fluid dairy division also has branch distribution operations in Watertown, Aberdeen, Pierre, and Rapid City.

In addition to bottling fluid milk, the Land O'Lakes plant in Sioux Falls distributes cottage cheese, sour cream, yogurt, fruit juices, and frozen desserts for South Dakota consumers. These products are just some of the more than 600 dairy foods products—including butter, cheese, and spreads—that Land O'Lakes markets to consumer, food service, and industrial customers all around the nation.

Surveys conducted by Land O'Lakes show that 98 percent of consumers in the United States recognize the Land O'Lakes brand name.

The Fluid Dairy Division's colorful semitrailer trucks display this nostalgic farm scene celebrating the Land O'Lakes heritage of "Good Things From The Land."

Other Land O'Lakes Dairy Foods plants located in South Dakota include the company's Alpine Lace plant in Sturgis, which packages deli cheese; and a cheese plant in Volga, which processes mozzarella.

Land O'Lakes has a strong agricultural services presence in South Dakota, with joint venture feed mills in Gettysburg and Sioux Falls, as well as a number of agronomy distribution centers across the state. Land O'Lakes agricultural services provide feed, seed, plant food, and crop protection products to more than 300,000 farmers and ranchers in 30 states. It provides these products and services mainly through a network of 1,100 locally owned and locally controlled farmer cooperatives across the United States.

Since its founding in 1921, Land O'Lakes has been a leader and innovator in dairy foods and agricultural services. Its vision over the years has remained consistent—Land O'Lakes is determined to be true to its heritage of serving farmer-cooperative members and delighting customers as it works to be one of the best food and agricultural companies in the world.

RETAIL & WHOLESALE >>

THE EMPIRE/EMPIRE EAST

The Empire (pictured at left) along with its sister center, Empire East, is the largest shopping complex in South Dakota, encompassing more than 1.4 million square feet of retail stores and attracting more than 14 million visitors annually.

The Empire/Empire East, the largest shopping center between Minneapolis and Denver, is one of the "sturdy oaks" in South Dakota's retail landscape.

Each year more than 14 million visitors make The Empire/Empire East one of the most popular tourist attractions in the state. Retailers at the regional shopping mall account for a majority of annual retail sales in Sioux Falls.

Construction of The Empire began on what was then a barely paved 41st Street—today it is a seven-lane thoroughfare. The shopping center was opened in September 1975 with nearly 600,000 square feet of space and 47 retail outlets. A dining court featuring several food vendors was opened in 1983.

The Empire/Empire East features 180 of the area's finest stores and restaurants to satisfy every shopper. As well as being a premier shopping destination, The Empire/ Empire East serves as a gathering place, hosting many events and programs that enhance the community and provide entertainment for visitors.

A ONE-STOP SHOPPING OASIS

Through several expansions, the center today has 180 stores and restaurants in 1.1 million square feet of space on nearly 130 acres. Major department store retailers such as Younkers, JCPenney, Dayton's, and Sears, plus a broad cross-section of premier speciality shops, make the center a one-stop shopping oasis for patrons.

With the addition of Empire East in 1988, the mall was expanded not only in size but also in its wider offering of retailers. Empire East, which is across the street from The Empire, was completely renovated to match the architecture of the existing Empire Mall. Major anchor retailers include Target and Kohl's. A main feature of Empire East—in addition to its eight large retail outlets—is a motion picture complex that shows first-run films and regularly attracts thousands of patrons.

With its convenient location at the intersection of Interstate 29 and 41st Street in Sioux Falls, The Empire/Empire East has become a focal point for South Dakota retailing—and a major boon to the economy. The shopping center is among the city's leading employers.

The Empire/Empire East, which is continuously being updated and expanded, offers a successful retail concept and attracts the most sought-after stores to service South Dakota and neighboring states.

CHAPTER TEN

GETTING THE WORD OUT

Given South Dakotans' passion for new technologies, it is not surprising to discover that television came along relatively early, in 1953, when KELO began broadcasting in Sioux Falls. At that time, almost everything was done with secondhand equipment. Lacking gear for live transmissions, the station *filmed* newscasts, then raced the reels to the transmitter for broadcasting. The pioneering spirit was alive and well in those early TV years.

Today television envelops us. CBS affiliate KELO, the big player, blankets eastern South Dakota and extends into Minnesota, Iowa, and Nebraska. Its Pierre and Rapid City outposts cover the rest of the state, as well as bits of North Dakota and Montana.

More than a dozen stations broadcast here, mainly from Sioux Falls and Rapid City. Sioux Falls' leading stations are KELO, KSFY, and KDLT. Rapid City has KELO, KCLO, KOTA, KEVN, and others. Major networks are well represented: ABC, CBS, and NBC, plus PBS and newcomers FOX, UPN, and WB.

DOWN THE WIRE
The cabling of South Dakota began in earnest in the early 1970s. Today, coaxial carries movie channels, "superstations," news outlets, and home shopping venues to every corner of the state. The lead actors are Denver-based TCI (Tele-Communications, Inc.) in the west and Midcontinent Communications in the east. Midcontinent has been a force to be reckoned with for half a century. It was KELO-TV's original owner, selling it only in the 1990s. Today Midcontinent owns numerous radio stations and is active in telecommunications, the Internet, and of course, cable television.

PHOTO: © Eric R. Berndt/Midwestock

VOX POPULI
South Dakota's public-broadcasting tradition is impressive. Educational television, as it was then known, began in 1961 with a low-power station at the University of South Dakota. Through the 1960s and 1970s, the state built seven additional stations, effectively covering the state's 77,116 square miles. The educational roots of public television still run deep. Much of the daytime weekday schedule consists of instructional programming aimed at schoolchildren.

UP AND DOWN THE DIAL
KELO began as an AM radio station in the 1930s and, with friendly rival KSOO, dominated the Sioux Falls market. But both were dwarfed by WNAX in Yankton. *Everyone* was dwarfed by WNAX. In the 1920s and 1930s, the FCC authorized a few extra-high-wattage stations in rural America, to reach remote locales, and WNAX was one of them. Even today its signal

As part of ABC's "Children First" campaign, Sioux Falls affiliate KSFY-TV has produced original programming to increase public awareness of the issues facing South Dakota children today.

covers about one-quarter million square miles, more than any other station in the United States.

Currently South Dakota has almost one hundred radio stations. Again, Midcontinent, with KELO-AM and its FM sibling, has been an unbeatable ratings force for decades, becoming an even greater powerhouse in the 1990s, when it acquired KRRO-FM, KWSN-AM, and KTWB-FM.

Public broadcasting is also well represented on the dial. The South Dakota Public Radio system consists of nine stations broadcasting local, National Public Radio, American Public Radio, and other programming around the clock. St. Paul–based Minnesota Public Radio has established itself here, too, with KRSD in Sioux Falls.

THE FRONT PAGE
South Dakota has a long newspaper tradition, extending back to the *Weekly Dakotan,* published at Yankton beginning June 6, 1861. South Dakotans are loyal toward their publications, too: The *Weekly Dakotan* still exists today, as the *Daily Press and Dakotan.*

Rapid City, South Dakota's second fastest growing urban center, is the home of the widely respected Rapid City Journal.

Today South Dakota boasts no fewer than 11 daily newspapers, plus more than 100 weeklies, and innumerable shoppers, specialty publications, and "freebies." National dailies such as *USA Today* (founded, incidentally, by South Dakota native Al Neuharth), the *New York Times,* and the *Wall Street Journal* are well entrenched locally. The *Denver Post,* the *Minneapolis Star Tribune,* and the *Omaha World-Herald* are obligatory reading in various corners of the state.

WE WERE THERE
The oldest continuously published newspaper in South Dakota, the *Yankton Daily Press and Dakotan,* began publication as the *Weekly Dakotan* 28 years before South Dakota became a state. Its pages reported such events as the South Dakota gold rush and Custer's defeat at Little Bighorn.

Considered the state's most important local dailies are the *Sioux Falls Argus Leader* and the *Rapid City Journal.* Both have readership and influence beyond their respective city limits. The *Argus Leader,* a component of the Gannett media empire, is seen by some 51,585 readers every day, 74,500 on Sundays. The *Journal* reaches 32,514 readers on weekdays, 36,500 on Sundays.

Other influential dailies are *Capital Journal* of Pierre (circulation 4,686), the *Watertown Public Opinion* (14,522), Aberdeen's *American News* (17,582 daily, 19,500 Sunday), and the *Huron Plainsman* (9,241 daily, 10,020 Sunday). Add to these the *Daily Press and Dakotan* (8,478), and we see that even in this electronic age the dailies hold their own, sometimes even increasing readership.

Weekly papers are popular in smaller communities. There are well over 100 such journals, ranging in circulation from a few hundred (the *Delmont Record,* with 250) to a few thousand (the *Mobridge Tribune* boasts 3,674). Given the sheer number of them, plus strong support of local readers and advertisers, the weeklies' future is virtually guaranteed.

KELO-TV has come a long way since its first news broadcast in 1953. Today you can get news on your computer screen, as well as your television screen, just by visiting http://www.kelotv.com. *KELO is one of at least four South Dakota television stations on the Internet. Others are KSFY, KDLT, and KOTA.*

EVERY MONTH OR TWO OR THREE

As early as 1899, Doane Robinson, the official state historian, "conducted" the *Monthly South Dakotan,* a general-interest magazine that continued well into the twentieth century. Today we publish at least two dozen periodicals, from the glossy, general-interest *South Dakota Magazine,* published at Yankton, to *South Dakota Review,* the University of South Dakota's literary publication, to *South Dakota Bird Notes,* published by the South Dakota Ornithologists' Union at Aberdeen. In between are various travel or outdoors publications—*Deadwood Magazine, Dakota Outdoors*—plus specialized periodicals such as *South Dakota Hall of Fame,* published at Fort Pierre.

MAKING BOOK

Book publishing here is vital and exciting. Many printing companies, including Pine Hill Press in Freeman and

Radio has brought news and culture into American homes for nearly eight decades. South Dakota had one of the earliest educational radio stations, KUSD-AM, which went on the air in the early 1920s, broadcasting from the University of South Dakota at Vermillion.

Sioux Falls, and State Publishing and Printing in Pierre and Rapid City, offer book production and binding. And there is an interesting small-press industry, too. The Center for Western Studies at Augustana College in Sioux Falls has published numerous titles—some scholarly, some not. Ex Machina Publishing, also in Sioux Falls, releases about one title a year, works ranging from satires to mysteries to historical volumes. Less energetic

AND THE REST IS HISTORY

In 1928 a young accordionist from North Dakota stopped at the new WNAX radio station in Yankton, hoping to make some money so he and his band could move on. The station manager fed them and put them on the air. Listener response to Lawrence Welk was so strong that his "one-night stand" lasted almost nine years.

schedules are maintained by the likes of East Eagle Company in Huron and Melius and Peterson in Aberdeen, original publisher of *My Book for Kids with Cansur* by then 10-year-old cancer survivor Jason Gaes.

WRITING THE FUTURE

A few Internet-based publications are cropping up, with most established journals and broadcasters having a cyberspace presence. This indicates continued expansion of South Dakota's communications media into the new millennium. Bridging the gap between far-flung residents has always been a priority in the Mount Rushmore State.

GET IT WHILE IT'S HOT

South Dakota Public Broadcasting is something of an Internet pioneer, having made a live feed of South Dakota Public Radio broadcasts available to "surfers" for some time now, and planning to add South Dakota Public Television's instructional programming as well as local weather information early in the new millennium.

COMMUNICATIONS >>

SOUTH DAKOTA NETWORK, INC.

Owned by

38 independent

telephone

companies,

South Dakota

Network, Inc.

(SDN), provides

state-of-the-art

telecommunications

services throughout

South Dakota

and beyond

South Dakota Network, Inc. (SDN), was incorporated in 1989 and is headquartered in Sioux Falls. Currently owned by 38 of the state's independent telephone companies, SDN was created to ensure that the rural areas of South Dakota would have access to state-of-the-art telecommunications services.

SDN and its owner local-exchange companies during 1998 and 1999 built the largest SONET (synchronous optical network) ring deployment in the upper Midwest. SONET ring technology protects the entire SDN network in case of service outages, whether caused by fiber cuts or acts of God, by simultaneously routing information both clockwise and counterclockwise around each ring; if there is a data loss, the system accesses its duplicate.

SDN is the state's most sophisticated provider of high-capacity and broadband information transport, and it has the capability to provide these services into more than 20 neighboring states as well. Additionally SDN markets frame relay; ATM (asynchronous transmission mode); IP (Internet protocol) telephony; IXC switching; LATA (local-access and transport-area)–specific terminating service; wholesale CLEC services; wholesale ISP (Internet service provisioning); SS7 (signaling system #7)

Symbolic of South Dakota Network's slogan, Transporting Information at the Speed of Light, is a bundle of fiber-optic strands that can carry an infinite number of communications transactions simultaneously.

information services; WAN (wide area network) consulting; and information-transport services consulting.

SDN's 4,000-plus miles of buried fiber-optic cable intersects all the state's major urban areas and some 179 of its other communities, and SDN has fiber-optic entrance facilities into all contiguous states. The entire fiber-optic network is connected to the SDN SUPER NODE switching system at SDN headquarters. At this single location, interexchange carriers (IXCs), competitive local-exchange carriers (CLECs), and Internet service providers (ISPs) can interconnect with the system. The SDN network has created a virtual market of more than 250,000 commercial, medical, educational, governmental, and residential customers to whom such companies can sell their communication services.

SDN is committed to expanding and developing its network within South Dakota and contiguous states into the next millennium. Because of its state-of-the-art communications technology, SDN serves as one of South Dakota's truly significant tools for economic development. Now even smaller rural communities that are interconnected to this network can use its advanced telecommunications resources as a major sales point when attempting to attract new industry.

For additional information, visit the South Dakota Network Web site at www.sdnet.net.

William Janklow, governor of South Dakota (right), and Darrell Henderson, president of South Dakota Network (left), commemorate the lighting of SDN's first SONET (synchronous optical network) ring during the fourth quarter of 1998.

SDN
South Dakota
Network, Inc.

U S WEST COMMUNICATIONS

Location. Distance. Time. Once the obstacles to economic development and personal well-being, these barriers now are all but completely shattered through the use of telecommunications. U S WEST is proud of the role it has played to make this possible for the people, businesses, and communities of South Dakota.

U S WEST offers more than a century of innovation in communications. Its heritage is rooted in three companies that were part of the renowned Bell Telephone System—Northwestern Bell (the Bell company in South Dakota), Mountain Bell, and Pacific Northwest Bell.

There is strong evidence that the community of Deadwood, South Dakota, had the first Bell-licensed telephone exchange in the Northwestern Bell region. This exchange opened between March and August of 1878, just two years after Alexander Graham Bell invented the telephone—and several months before even the White House telephone, installed in a wooden booth outside the oval office, could be used by President Rutherford B. Hayes.

Telephone service spread rapidly across South Dakota. An exchange was opened in Yankton in 1881 and in Rapid City by 1882. Residents of Sioux Falls also could order telephone service in 1882, and by 1886 pioneer J. L. W. Zietlow was operating an independent telephone exchange in Aberdeen with 65 subscribers. The following year, telephone service was extended to Huron, Milbank, Sisseton, and other smaller South Dakota towns.

By 1897 New Yorkers could make telephone calls all the way to South Dakota for the pricey sum of

The U S WEST Communications South Dakota headquarters is located at 125 South Dakota Avenue in downtown Sioux Falls.

ten dollars. In 1915 coast-to-coast calls became a reality. They were partly enabled by the vacuum tube—invented by Iowan Lee De Forest and perfected by Bell scientists—which played a major role in amplifying sound over long distances.

In 1909 the Northwestern Group of Bell Telephone Companies was established. Its principals were the Northwestern Telephone Exchange Company (operating in the Dakotas and Minnesota), the Iowa Company, and the Nebraska Company (which had several exchanges in South Dakota).

In January 1921 the three companies in the Northwestern Group were merged to form Northwestern Bell. Later that same year, dial telephones began appearing in Northwestern Bell–served towns, allowing people to complete local calls without operator assistance.

For the next seven decades, Northwestern Bell worked hard to make modern telephone service available to customers in urban and rural areas.

In 1927 it introduced the first telephone with a handset, and in 1940 it produced a business telephone equipped with six buttons for pick-up or transfer of calls. In the 1950s color telephones became available and in the 1960s Trimline telephones, Direct Distance (1+) Dialing, Touch-Tone calling, and WATS service were introduced. In

U S WEST features a national directory-assistance center in South Dakota. Customers can call 411 to obtain any listed phone number in any area code in the nation.

1971 Northwestern Bell's first Traffic Service Position System (TSPS) electronic operator consoles were installed in Sioux Falls, allowing callers to dial person-to-person and collect (0+) calls. South Dakota also was the first state in Northwestern Bell's territory to have a statewide directory-assistance center, and the first state in the nation to use Western Electric's computerized HILO Electronic Switching System, a local and long-distance call-switching system.

More than 36,000 miles of fiber-optic lines have been installed in South Dakota by U S WEST, increasing the power of the company's telecommunications network.

By the 1960s advances in technology and employee dedication enabled Northwestern Bell to achieve an industrywide goal—universal telephone service; that is, universally available and affordable service.

On January 1, 1984, through the court-directed Bell system divestiture, Northwestern Bell, which had been owned by AT&T, became a subsidiary of U S WEST, Inc., in Denver, Colorado. It was given its new name, U S WEST Communications, on July 1, 1988.

U S WEST employs more than 600 people in South Dakota and provides telecommunications services to more than 250,000 customer lines in 100 towns. Proud of its century-long legacy in the telephone business, U S WEST is even more proud of the new legacy it is building in the information age.

Since 1988 U S WEST has invested more than $400 million in South Dakota to build a premier telecommunications network. The company has more than 36,000 miles of fiber-optic lines in place and is routinely adding more. All of the communities it serves are connected with digital facilities. All customers have access to digital call-switching systems and popular telephone features such as Call Waiting and Caller ID.

U S WEST has deployed backup systems that are designed to quickly fix system problems—often before customers realize there is a problem. The company maintains diverse toll routes across the state and has completed two large SONET (synchronous optical network) fiber-optic rings that together cover most of the U S WEST eastern South Dakota service area. The strength of these rings is that any break is instantly rectified; if a transmission fails, SONET rings carry the signal through in another direction.

This multifaceted, state-of-the-art infrastructure is the foundation on which U S WEST is building an advanced digital network for delivery of electronic commerce, telemedicine, and distance-learning telecommunications.

U S WEST has equipped its network for frame relay service, which sends data in packets, for high-speed transmission. Frame relay is offered in all U S WEST South Dakota exchanges and is being used to serve business, education, and government high-speed communication needs.

U S WEST also is deploying faster technology for Internet access. It was the first company in the nation to launch digital subscriber line (DSL) technology on a wide-scale commercial basis. DSL converts copper telephone lines into express lanes for high-speed Internet use. In the first multicity deployment of this technology, the switching systems serving Sioux Falls were upgraded to offer U S WEST's DSL services, which are called "MegaBit."

Another U S WEST investment that will benefit South Dakota well into the future is the expansion of asynchronous transfer mode (ATM) technology. U S WEST has committed more than $6.5 million in 1999 to expand its use of ATM, which provides ultra-fast information-transfer capability. ATM serves applications that require real-time data, video, and audio transfers, such as telemedicine, multimedia distance learning, and advanced scientific research projects.

The former Bell Telephone Company has come a long way from the days it provided simple telephone service and telephone books. U S WEST now offers telecommunications products and technology that make life better in South Dakota—that have shattered the barriers of location, distance, and time.

Millions of dollars are invested in equipment and services every year by U S WEST so the firm can bring new services and technology to its South Dakota customers.

CHAPTER ELEVEN

HEAD OF THE CLASS

In 1999 Dakota State University in Madison (DSU) clocked in at number 10 on *Yahoo! Internet Life* magazine's list of the 100 most wired colleges in the United States. In part, this goes back to South Dakotans' love of technology. DSU is almost completely wired: The school handles virtually all administrative functions electronically; it requires Internet training of all students and faculty; all its classes feature on-line materials; 85 percent of the

classes incorporate on-line work; and the school is a regional pioneer in distance learning. Best of all, the computer lab waiting period is less than 15 minutes.

This national distinction for DSU also reflects our long-standing love affair with education. Even before statehood, South Dakota's pioneers drafted a plan to create school lands and preserve them into the future, a plan in force yet today. Establishing some sort of school was a top priority for every wave of settlers. The abandoned remains of some of these one-room schoolhouses remain on the landscape today.

No wonder the Mount Rushmore State leads the nation in high school graduation rates: Nearly 90 percent of those who enter South Dakota high schools subsequently exit with a diploma in hand (the national average is less than 70 percent). Of those who graduate, more than 35 percent will go on to finish at least one year of postsecondary education.

Schools project had only one district left to go. And "wiring" doesn't mean one computer lab with Internet access; it means every classroom, lab, library, and administrative office in every school. Guidelines call for three cables for every four students, ensuring access for all users with minimal "buddying up." Once the last public school district is brought on-line, the nine full-time wiring crews will move on to private elementary and secondary schools, public libraries, and public universities.

Meanwhile, a second initiative, the Connecting the Schools project, dovetails with Wiring the Schools by linking all public schools—again, kindergarten through high school—into a single intranet, the first of its kind in the United States. This will provide distance learning, E-mail and Web hosting services; file servers and software; and conferencing capabilities across the state.

CABLES IN THE CLASSROOM

Universities have no monopoly on technology in South Dakota. In the 1990s, Governor William Janklow spearheaded an ambitious undertaking to wire every public school in the state. By the end of 1998, the Wiring the

Small classes and a dedicated faculty contribute to Augustana College's fine academic reputation. Ninety percent of Augustana's graduating seniors who enter the workplace find jobs in their fields within six months. In the class of 1998, every computer science, MIS, nursing, and accounting graduate found employment.

PHOTO: *Courtesy, Augustana College*

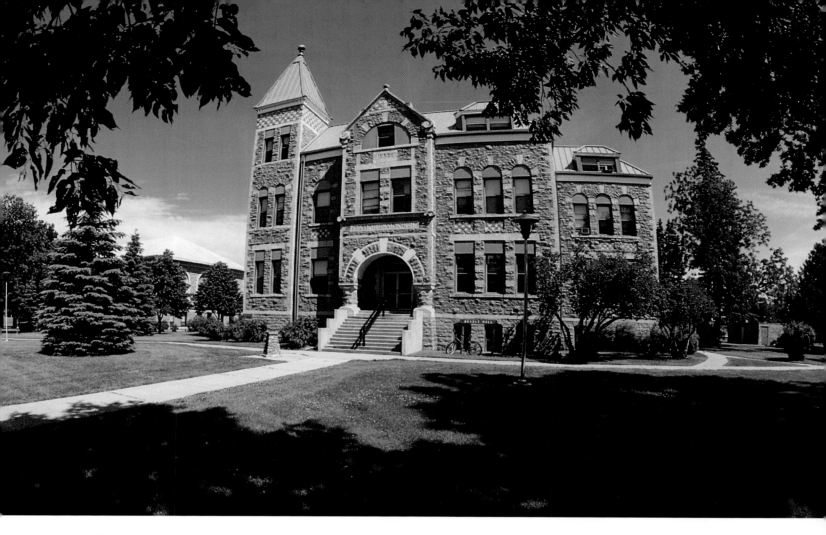

When these projects are finished, South Dakota will have the most wired school system in the nation, bar none. This will not only provide the state's youngsters with a valuable educational tool today, but will also prepare them for their increasingly computerized tomorrow.

MEANWHILE, BACK ON CAMPUS

Wiring the Schools and Connecting the Schools will also prepare our kids for the increasingly digital world of higher education. Dakota State University may be "computer central" among the state's universities, but it is not alone in that brave new world.

Currently, half a dozen institutions comprise the state university system. In addition to DSU, there are the flagships: South Dakota State University, at Brookings, founded by the Territorial Legislature in 1881 and today the state's largest university; and the University of South Dakota, at Vermillion, created a year later. Between them, they offer well over 200 majors, plus graduate and professional schools.

The system of four-year universities is completed by Black Hills State University, at Spearfish; Northern State University, at Aberdeen; and South Dakota School of Mines and Technology, at Rapid City. These institutions

Dakota State University's Beadle Hall is a picturesque reminder that DSU exists not only in cyberspace, despite its "wired" image. Recently DSU students made a brick-and-mortar commitment to their community: Money from an increase in activity fees agreed to by DSU students is helping to build the new Madison Community Center, a recreational facility for all area residents, with subsidized memberships planned for those with low income.

cover the state geographically and offer a wide range of subjects, from business, medicine, and law at USD to agriculture, nursing, and pharmacy at SDSU to education at Northern to engineering at the School of Mines, and more.

LAYING THE GROUNDWORK

The Wiring the Schools project is an example of a win-win situation. The benefits to schools are obvious. But the crews doing the wiring consist of South Dakota state prison inmates. These carefully screened "trusties" are gaining important hands-on training that they can put to good use when they return to society.

Of the state's private colleges and universities, Augustana College, a Lutheran institution in Sioux Falls, takes top honors. "Augie" is routinely touted as one of the best small colleges in the region, a reputation substantiated by *U.S. News & World Report,* which ranked the school at number eight in its top 10 list of midwestern liberal arts colleges in both 1998 and 1999.

Other private colleges and universities include the University of Sioux Falls (until recently known as Sioux Falls College); Dakota Wesleyan University, at Mitchell; Mount Marty College, at Yankton; Presentation College, at Aberdeen; National American University, at Rapid City; Sinte Gleska University at Rosebud; Oglala Lakota College, at Kyle; and Huron University, at Huron. Having more than a dozen accredited four-year colleges and universities in a state with a small population speaks volumes about the importance South Dakotans place on education.

We should mention, too, that a given university's mailing address is becoming less and less important. The growing trend toward distance learning is well at home here in the Mount Rushmore State, with virtually all public institutions onboard or soon to be.

LET'S GET TECHNICAL

Another trend in the Mount Rushmore State is nontraditional education. South Dakotans saw that train coming more than 30 years ago, and met it with a state network of technical schools that is today growing almost faster than administrators can build new parking lots. This

Governor Janklow's Connecting the Schools project is creating an intranet for children and teens in all South Dakota schools, which will not only give students access to course offerings anywhere in the state, but will help little cyber-surfers such as these develop early mastery of the tools they need to keep pace with a changing world of information.

PHOTO: © Michael Krasowitz/FPG International LLC

consortium consists of Lake Area Technical Institute, at Watertown; Western Dakota Technical Institute, at Rapid City; Mitchell Technical Institute, at Mitchell; and the largest, Southeast Technical Institute, at Sioux Falls. These schools offer certificate programs and two-year associate degree programs in an almost overwhelming array of course offerings, including biotechnology, medical lab technology, banking and finance, computer information processing, agriculture chemical technology, satellite communications, computer-aided drafting, and dozens more.

A further testament to the richness of this field is the existence in South Dakota of the private Colorado Technical University. The university arrived in Sioux Falls only a few years ago, but it has already built a new campus where computers and other high-tech course offerings are emphasized.

CROSSROADS OF THE INFORMATION HIGHWAY

As the new millennium approaches it is interesting to note how two areas close to South Dakotans' hearts, education

Researchers at the South Dakota School of Mines and Technology's "Big Pig Dig," in Badlands National Park, uncover the remains of ruminating pigs called oreodons and other prehistoric mammals.

and high technology, have overlapped. Our already high educational standards and enviable quality of education will only be bolstered by increasing utilization of cutting-edge technology in the future. But history clearly indicates that the focus will remain on the students.

NEW TOOLS OF THE TRADE

Noting that computer skills have become a top priority with employers, Sioux Falls' Southeast Technical Institute has begun to equip students and instructors in computer information systems studies—as well as electronics and certain engineering programs—with IBM Thinkpad 380XD laptop computers, fully integrating the computers into the curricula.

SOUTH DAKOTA TECHNICAL INSTITUTES

SOUTH DAKOTA

TECHNICAL INSTITUTES

IN MITCHELL,

RAPID CITY,

SIOUX FALLS, AND

WATERTOWN, OFFER

STATE-OF-THE-ART

EDUCATION IN

MORE THAN 70

DEGREE/DIPLOMA

PROGRAMS

With a focus on twenty-first-century technology, the South Dakota Technical Institutes have played a major role in the economic development of the state. Founded in the mid-1960s as training resources, the technical institutes have evolved to become a strong economic force for the state of South Dakota.

Technical training in South Dakota is offered on four separate campuses across the state: Mitchell Technical Institute, in Mitchell; Western Dakota Technical Institute, in Rapid City; Southeast Technical Institute, in Sioux Falls; and Lake Area Technical Institute, in Watertown. Each campus offers associate degrees, diplomas, and certificates in a wide range of program areas.

Program divisions include: agriculture, business, food services, health occupations, office technologies, and trade and technical studies. Together, the technical schools offer more than 70 degree/diploma programs that apply state-of-the-art technology in support of the curricula. Moreover, the geographic diversity of the institutes enhances employment opportunities for graduates.

One of the most attractive features of the technical institutes is their procedural and instructional ties with business and industry. Each program is tailored to meet industry requirements as a result of careful guidance and suggestions from representative advisory committees. The advisory committees are composed of professionals from industries that are most likely to hire program graduates. Comments, questions, and actions set forth by advisory committee members keep each technical area

Some of the latest manufacturing and machining technology is available to students at all four South Dakota Technical Institutes, including Lake Area Technical Institute, in Watertown.

current with industry and honed for the technology of the future.

As businesses and the technical institutes act jointly to provide high-quality education for students, advisory committee involvement has led to the upgrade of current programs as well as the creation of new programs. At the state level, the connection between industry and the technical schools has been acknowledged through special funding programs. Funds have been specifically appropriated to enable the schools to purchase the latest equipment and to update facilities to stay well ahead of technological advances.

The end result is an effective, mutually beneficial partnership of state, school, and industry,

Team projects at the four institutes encourage cooperation, communication, and leadership. These students are creating a merchandising exhibit at Western Dakota Technical Institute, in Rapid City.

MITCHELL TECHNICAL INSTITUTE

which enhances the capabilities, possibilities, and opportunities for all involved. Some of the programs created through the guidance of advisory committees have drawn national recognition and are being used as models for similar programs across the United States.

In addition to support for the schools, many businesses also provide encouragement and support for students. Internships are made available to students while they are attending school. Special scholarships from businesses have been created and targeted for technical students. At graduation such businesses are able to reap the benefits of their support by hiring highly trained, ready-to-work graduates. More than 80 percent of all technical institute graduates remain in South Dakota, taking advantage of the employment opportunities available throughout the state.

The technical institutes all have a similar mission: to provide high-quality, up-to-date technical training and encourage lifelong learning. Hundreds of outstanding instructors lead the way in meeting these goals. Every program area is taught in

All four technical institutes have an area of specialty. At Mitchell Technical Institute the satellite technology program remains on the cutting edge.

a hands-on setting by instructors who have extensive on-the-job experience. The practical experience of the instructors helps students become acutely aware of expectations in the field. This educational approach has drawn national recognition and has been a key reason that the four technical schools have experienced steady growth over the past decade.

RETRAINING OPPORTUNITIES

In addition to training new professionals, the technical institutes also facilitate retraining opportunities for businesses statewide. Through the Business and Industry Training Centers located at each technical school, businesses are able to boost productivity of their current staff members through exposure to advanced technology or new business concepts. Among the most popular of these retraining programs at present is computer software training. However, additional retraining opportunities exist in virtually every technical area offered by the schools.

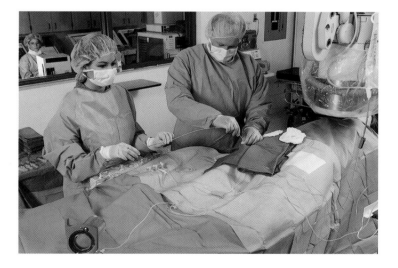

Students work in true-to-life environments as they obtain hands-on experience. These cardiovascular students at Southeast Technical Institute in Sioux Falls benefit from this state-of-the-art opportunity.

AUGUSTANA COLLEGE

Dating back to 1860, Augustana College was founded by Lars P. Esbjorn to educate young men in the holy ministry in the Lutheran faith. Over the years the college has been located in three midwestern states. (At one time Augustana was referred to as the "College on Wheels.") In 1918, however, the college became a permanent fixture of the South Dakota community, putting down roots in Sioux Falls.

Augustana's theme for many years has been "Enter to learn, leave to serve." The recently completed Augustana Renewal Campaign has provided the college with a solid foundation for the future. The most ambitious fund-raising campaign in the history of the college, Augustana Renewal was conducted over five years and raised more than $40 million.

The Augustana College Administration Building, completed in 1920, is the gateway to the college's 100-acre Sioux Falls campus.

In the nearly 140 years since the college was founded, thousands of Augustana graduates have gone on to serve the nation, the state, and the local community. Many of the region's best and brightest students have become major influences in the cultural and economic growth of the area. In Sioux Falls alone more than 200 teachers and 80 of the city's physicians have degrees from Augustana.

Augustana students have the opportunity to assist in important research.

The college annually awards undergraduate degrees to more than 300 young people. These undergraduate degrees span 44 separate disciplines and 14 preprofessional programs. In addition to providing the region with many of its leaders, Augustana is now an international institution. Students from 12 nations attend classes in Sioux Falls. During the 1998–1999 academic year the famed Augustana Concert Band toured Asia. Moreover, during the college's January interim many faculty members teach abroad.

With an academic planning process that involves input from the Board of Regents, campus faculty and leadership, students, and alumni, Augustana established criteria for daily

decisions and planning, called the "five fundamental values":

- Christian: With identity rooted in the church, Augustana is committed to being a college of the Evangelical Lutheran Church in America (ELCA).
- Liberal Arts: Augustana is a college of the liberal arts by providing an education of enduring worth.
- Community: The college's enrollment is knit together in a community of people that care for, respect, and empower one another and tend to the ecology of place.
- Excellence: The Augustana College community is committed to excellence in teaching, learning, supporting, and administering.
- Service: The campus community accepts the call to servanthood and service and affirms that wholeness includes reaching out to each other.

With a campus that already encompasses 100 acres, Augustana is expanding to accommodate the waves of students expected to enroll in the twenty-first century.

Approximately 25 percent of Augustana's students participate in the college's outstanding music program.

The Madsen Social Science Center was completed in the spring of 1999. The building complex replaces a World War II structure that served Augustana for more than 50 years. The Madsen Center will provide expanded and technology-capable space for both students and faculty in the college's largest division.

In addition, the Edith Mortenson Center is being converted to a center for theater and student services, and a new Center for Western Studies is on the drawing board, expanding one of the college's fastest-growing educational disciplines.

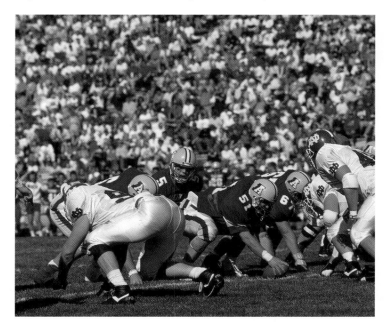

Augustana is one of the few colleges of the ELCA in the United States to compete in NCAA Division II athletics.

ENTER TO LEARN
LEAVE TO SERVE

For nearly 140 years Augustana College has been committed to preparing tomorrow's leaders to meet the challenges of the years ahead.

For additional information please contact Augustana College at 2001 South Summit Avenue, Sioux Falls, South Dakota 57197

CHAPTER TWELVE

A STATE OF GOOD HEALTH

South Dakota has the nation's second highest number of hospital beds per 1,000 population. And a stay in one of those beds will cost you less than at anyplace else in the United States: $476 per inpatient day. As with most rural states, South Dakota's remote regions face ongoing challenges in attracting and keeping physicians and other health care professionals. But in general, South Dakotans enjoy readily available health care that is second to none.

HIGH-TECH ADVANTAGE

South Dakota has embraced all kinds of advances in medical technology. With residents scattered across a sizable landscape, technology for bringing patients and doctors together has been, literally, a life-saver. The still-new field of telemedicine ensures access to quality health care for people in even isolated areas. Through such initiatives as Medical Ultrasound Three-dimensional Portable Advanced Communication (MUSTPAC), an obstetrician with McKennan Health Services in Sioux Falls can consult real-time with a colleague at, say, Pine Ridge as both simultaneously view an ultrasound image. This reduces travel costs and expenses for patients and more fully extends the services of South Dakota's major medical centers to smaller, more distant portions of the state.

Sometimes the technology goes to the patient. Major hospitals in South Dakota, through alliances with one another and with smaller hospitals, actually take medical technology to smaller hospitals and clinics that can't afford them. It is commonplace to see the magnetic resonance imaging unit jointly owned by Sioux Falls hospitals en route to a small town.

CHECKING INTO HOSPITALS

The major medical centers are in the major population centers. Rapid City Regional Hospital is at the heart of a system that serves the Black Hills region and most of western South Dakota, plus portions of Montana, Wyoming, Nebraska, and North Dakota. This system includes several hospitals, nursing home and assisted-living facilities, and clinics.

At the other end of the state, Sioux Falls' two general hospitals have conspired to create a significant regional medical center. Avera McKennan Hospital and Sioux Valley Hospital offer services and procedures that, until recently, required patients to travel to Minneapolis, Rochester, or Denver. Cardiovascular, orthopedic, cancer, and severe-burn treatments in particular bring patients from across the upper Midwest to South Dakota's largest city.

But like Rapid City Regional, the Sioux Falls institutions are more than just hospitals: They too are ground

Children's Care Hospital and School (CCHS) serves more than 1,400 children with disabilities and chronic health conditions. Shown here are staff members at CCHS's Rapid City outreach center.

zero for far-flung, diverse health care systems. Avera McKennan is the flagship of Avera Health, formerly Presentation Health System, a regional network serving eastern South Dakota as well as parts of Iowa, Minnesota, and Nebraska. Avera Health includes more than a dozen hospitals. Among them are Avera McKennan, Avera St. Luke's in Aberdeen, Avera Queen of Peace in Mitchell, and Avera Sacred Heart in Yankton—plus clinics, long-term care facilities, home care companies, assisted-living centers, and more. Avera McKennan has staked a claim in cancer and burn treatments, and is at the vanguard of women's health, children's health, and wellness.

So, too, is Sioux Valley Hospital, centerpiece of Sioux Valley Health System, which also covers most of eastern South Dakota with associated hospitals and clinics. Noted for cardiovascular care, Sioux Valley also constructed one of the first wellness centers in the region: Sioux Valley Wellness Center. Now Avera has entered this arena with its McKennan Center for Health & Fitness, also in Sioux Falls.

The largest multispecialty clinic in the upper Midwest, Central Plains Clinic prides itself on high-quality, personalized care.

THIS IS SPECIAL

Health care in South Dakota is marked by several specialty hospitals and care providers. Chief among these is Children's Care Hospital and School (CCHS), based in Sioux Falls with outreach centers in Rapid City and Mobridge. Until recently known as Crippled Children's

HEALTHY NUMBERS

Nationally speaking, South Dakota has the second highest number of community hospitals per 100,000 population and nearly twice the average number of hospital beds per 1,000 population. The state can also boast the second lowest average cost to hospitals per patient in the country.

The first set of quintuplets on record to live more than five years were born to Mr. and Mrs. Andrew J. Fischer of Aberdeen. James Andrew, Mary Ann, Mary Catherine, Mary Magdalen, and Mary Margaret were delivered on September 14, 1963, at Saint Luke's Hospital by Dr. James Barbos.

Hospital and School, the 45-year-old CCHS treats kids with chronic health problems and disabilities, and provides support services for their families. CCHS is not only a care facility but also a school—certified by the South Dakota Department of Education—and a home for its young clients.

The Good Samaritan Society, a non-profit network of nursing homes and assisted living centers, has its national headquarters in Sioux Falls. Catering to the elderly and others in need, the Society began in 1922 when a priest raised money to help a boy struck by polio. The organization today has facilities in 25 states.

Sioux Valley Behavioral Health is one of the state's best-known entities in the expanding field of psychiatric and behavioral health care. Avera McKennan has long been involved in that area, too. In addition, the publicly owned Yankton State Hospital is a regional leader in treatment of psychiatric and drug-related problems.

South Dakota is also garnering a reputation as a center for refractive surgery—procedures that enable people to see well without corrective lenses. Vance Thompson, M.D., of Ophthalmology Ltd. in Sioux Falls is a nationally renowned and widely published expert in the field, and maintains a busy schedule consulting patients on the pros and cons

of radial keratotomy, photorefractive keratectomy, LASIK surgery, and other state-of-the-art procedures.

Outpatient surgery facilities have proliferated in recent years, in line with the national trend. Rapid City's Same Day Surgery Center, L.L.C., and Sioux Falls Surgical Center, plus corresponding departments in many hospitals, give consumers in the Mount Rushmore State more options and greater control over their own health care choices than ever before.

WHITHER HMOS?
South Dakotans have been slow to join the national trend in health maintenance organizations (HMOs). As of this writing only one HMO operates in South Dakota: DAKOTACARE. As a managed care organization,

Part of the region's largest health system, Avera McKennan Hospital has more than 400 beds and is home to a cancer institute, children's facility, diabetes center, and certified trauma center.

PHOTO: © Eric R. Berndt/Midwestock

DIGITAL ROLL CALL

Another merging of high technology and health care is found on the Internet, in the form of Cradle Roll, funded by the Sioux Valley Foundation. Utilizing digital photography, Cradle Roll allows friends and family anywhere in the world to see newborns at Sioux Valley Hospital by going to www.siouxvalley.org/CradleRoll/index.htm.

organizations. Between them, DAKOTACARE and Wellmark seem to have cornered South Dakota's managed care market for the present.

GETTING HEALTHY, STAYING WELL

At the crossroads of the millennia, health care is an exciting growth industry in the Mount Rushmore State. And you get the feeling that the breathtaking explosion of health care options, facilities, technology, and providers is only beginning.

Paramedics at Sioux Valley Hospital and University Medical Center quickly load their helicopter before taking off to pick up a patient.

DAKOTACARE offers employers a number of different plans to cover clinic visits, hospitalization, pharmaceuticals, hospice care, and other health-related expenses. Unlike many HMOs, DAKOTACARE owns no clinics or care facilities; rather it works with and through the state's private system to provide benefits to its members.

Similarly, Wellmark Blue Cross Blue Shield of South Dakota provides health care coverage via employers, with traditional indemnity plans as well as preferred provider

HELP WHERE IT'S NEEDED MOST

The South Dakota Rural Telemedicine Project makes telemedicine services available to eight rural communities, which include six hospitals, three nursing homes, five primary care clinics, and three home health/hospice programs. It also provides consultation and medical education access. The Project especially targets the elderly, women, children, the disabled, minorities, and low-income groups.

THE GOOD SAMARITAN SOCIETY

At The Good Samaritan Society there is a family atmosphere among the residents and the staff.

The name alone conjures visions of one person helping another. It has become shorthand for any good deed or kind action. Headlines proclaim "Good Samaritan" deeds; articles document the circumstances of those deeds.

The roots of the term "Good Samaritan" are found in the Bible, in the tale of the traveler from Jerusalem who, on his way to Jericho, is beaten and robbed. The wounded traveler is aided by a passing Samaritan who comes upon him. While the Bible does not document who this Samaritan is, Jesus recognizes him as the "one who showed him [the wounded traveler] kindness," admonishing people to "go and do as he did."

Founded in 1922 by the Reverend August "Dad" Hoeger, The Good Samaritan Society evokes this 2,000-year-old beginning. Reflecting about the

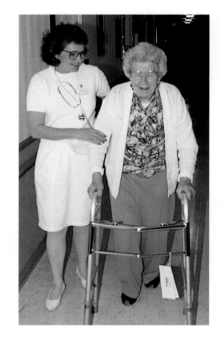

The nursing home facilities of The Good Samaritan Society offer a wide variety of choices and relationships for residents.

humble origins of The Good Samaritan Society, Hoeger observed, "I, of course, like to think that the whole Good Samaritan Society started in the heart of God; that it was His goodwill that His people should have Christian care and so He put into the hearts of men that they go and do His good pleasure." A parish pastor in North Dakota in the early 1920s, Hoeger raised funds to aid a young boy crippled by polio. The funds exceeded the need, and the extra money was used to help other handicapped individuals. To assure the continuation of these good works, The Evangelical Lutheran Good Samaritan Society was incorporated in North Dakota in 1922 as a religious, charitable, nonprofit corporation.

The first Good Samaritan Center opened in a rented six-room house in Arthur, North Dakota, the location of Hoeger's small-town ministry. By 1925 the house and an adjacent 40 acres had been purchased and a two-story dormitory erected; a third building was under construction.

The society grew beyond its original property, opening its headquarters in Fargo, North Dakota, and ultimately expanding during the Great Depression of the 1930s to facilities in 27 locations in 10 states. By 1962 the society operated 71 facilities in 13 states.

The society's headquarters was moved in 1963 from Fargo, North Dakota, to Sioux Falls, South Dakota. In early 1999 the name of the full campus was changed to The Evangelical Lutheran Good Samaritan Society National Campus. The main administration building

Residents of a Good Samaritan retirement community gather often for fellowship and fun.

was named The Hoeger Building to recognize the prominent role played by "Dad" Hoeger and his family. The building has been rededicated to provide resources and services that enable caregivers in the society's centers and communities to share God's love in word and deed.

Within the newly remodeled facilities at the campus, the Augusta Study enables staff and guests to study and meditate, celebrating the society's living commitment to Christian care and services. The study was named to honor the society's first caregiver,

Augusta Priewe, and all those who have followed her as caregivers. A new facility, The Jerstad Center, will provide Christ-centered leadership by meeting the educational needs of the society's staff and the long-term community. The center houses a chapel, a retreat center, classrooms, and distance-learning facilities.

The Hoeger name has remained integral to the society's heritage. Following his resignation, Hoeger was succeeded first by his son Augie and then by his son John, who was installed as president in 1987. When John Hoeger retired, the society named Dr. Mark Jerstad as president. Following Jerstad's death in 1997, Dr. Charles Balcer served as interim president. In 1998 Dr. Judith A. Ryan was installed as the society's president.

An official affiliate of the two major Lutheran Church bodies—the Evangelical Lutheran Church of America (ELCA) and Lutheran Church Missouri Synod (LCMS)— The Good Samaritan Society has carried on its 77-year traditions under Ryan. Today the society operates more than 240 facilities in 25 states, employs 23,600 staff members and serves

Good Samaritan cares for its residents—mind, body, and soul.

27,500 residents. A principal reason for the society's continuing success is a unique combination of faith, determination, and flexibility.

The Good Samaritan Society's mission statement succinctly chronicles its basic purpose and beliefs: The mission of The Evangelical Lutheran Good Samaritan Society is to share God's love in word and deed by providing shelter and supportive services to older persons and others in need, believing that "In Christ's Love, Everyone Is Someone."

The Good Samaritan National Campus in Sioux Falls serves as a resource for its long-term care facilities nationwide, which offer services ranging from skilled nursing-home care to independent living. The centers provide special care units for such illnesses as Alzheimer's, along with subacute care, respite care, and home health care. Residents can receive physical, occupational, speech/language, respiratory, intravenous, and outpatient therapies, as well as hospice and adult day care. For older persons who are functionally and socially independent a majority of the time, the centers provide congregate housing (meal service, housekeeping, transportation, and emergency services) and assisted living (maximum independence for residents who do not need skilled medical care). In addition, the centers provide HUD (Housing and Urban Development) units that are designed for the low-income elderly, including those who are mobility-impaired but who can care for their own daily needs.

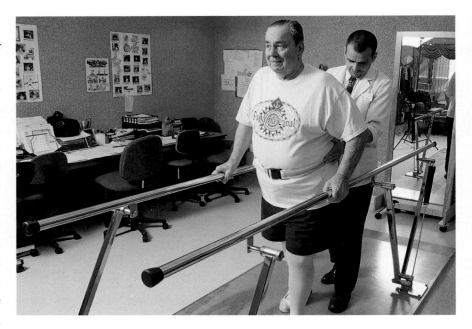

Good Samaritan skilled nursing facilities offer extensive rehabilitation, including physical, occupational, and speech/language therapies, as well as intravenous and respiratory care.

The society's national center in Sioux Falls brings together young and old, learning and housing, health care and wellness. The national center focuses on relationships—physical and spiritual, gathered and distant. Its four primary purposes are:

- To provide facilities and programs necessary to enrich the learning experience for staff who care for society residents. State-of-the-art telecommunications systems and technologies enhance learning both at the national center and at centers throughout the United States.
- To enable society staff to communicate and form partnerships more effectively with other organizations and colleagues throughout the long-term care profession.
- To provide a gathering place for society members and other national experts to share knowledge, examine issues, and develop solutions, programs, and systems for enhanced resident care.
- To provide the necessary base for support services required by the field-based needs of facilities in carrying out the society's mission in their respective communities.

The society continues to strive to fulfill its mission, remembering that "In Christ's Love, Everyone Is Someone."

Good Samaritan's hallmark values, which are focused on Christ, residents, staff, and community, are evident in the lives of the society's residents.

DAKOTACARE

The health care plan of the South Dakota Medical Association, DAKOTACARE, began operations in 1986 to provide the physicians of the state an opportunity to participate in the delivery and financing of health care and to give them an active role in the way managed care and its related procedures affect the medical practice.

The state's first and only statewide health maintenance organization (HMO) remains in the forefront of innovative product design, provider contracting and support, and effective, widely accepted medical management techniques.

DAKOTACARE has the largest and most comprehensive network of health care providers of any managed care organization in South Dakota, serving more than 80,000 members throughout the state and across the nation. More than 98 percent of the state's physicians, 100 percent of its hospitals, more than 95 percent of its pharmacies, plus hundreds of other providers of medical services participate in the organization's statewide network.

This unprecedented network offers maximum freedom of choice to members in their selection of health care providers and facilities.

DAKOTACARE, headquartered in Sioux Falls, has the largest, most comprehensive network of providers of any managed care organization in South Dakota.

DAKOTACARE™
THE HEALTH CARE PLAN OF THE SOUTH DAKOTA MEDICAL ASSOCIATION

The health care company in 1993 introduced the state of South Dakota's first combined managed care and claims administration for self-funded employers. This program was nominated for an ABEX Award in 1995 by the South Dakota Industry and Commerce Association for Best New South Dakota Product.

Among the many additional services offered by DAKOTACARE are group life insurance, long-term and short-term disability insurance, group universal life insurance, cancer and dread disease coverage, dental coverage, workers' compensation, COBRA and flexible benefits administration, long-term care insurance, Medicare supplements, and other wellness care, including the Mother-To-Be program.

Contact DAKOTACARE at 1323 South Minnesota Avenue, Sioux Falls, South Dakota 57105; telephone (605) 334-4000 or (800) 325-5598; fax: (605) 336-0270; or visit the company's Web site at www.dakotacare.com for more information.

The health care providers of DAKOTACARE serve more than 80,000 members in the state of South Dakota and throughout the United States.

CENTRAL PLAINS CLINIC

With more than 110 physicians on staff, Central Plains Clinic stands as one of the largest multispecialty clinics located in the upper Midwest.

At Central Plains Clinic the team of medical professionals is dedicated to providing the highest quality care to those they serve. By working one-on-one with one another, the physicians and staff are able to accurately diagnose and effectively treat patients who are faced with an extensive range of health issues.

With five locations in Sioux Falls, including Central Plains Clinic Main, East Primary Care Clinic, West Primary Care Clinic, Pulmonary Medicine Clinic and Oncology/Hematology Clinic, Central Plains Clinic health care services are conveniently accessed throughout the city. In addition Central Plains Clinic has a rural health location in Beresford and regional centers in

both Watertown and Rapid City. Central Plains Clinic strives to be the most comprehensive, convenient, and committed health care provider in South Dakota.

A BROAD RANGE OF SPECIALTIES

Central Plains Clinic offers exceptional primary and specialty care as well as comprehensive therapeutic and diagnostic support services. The team of medical professionals also offers services to employers throughout the state in prevention and cost containment of work-related injuries. By assisting the employer in establishing the baseline medical and physical status of their employees, Central Plains Clinic helps to identify and document pre-existing injuries and impairments.

Through a combination of high-quality equipment and state-of-the-art technology, Central Plains Clinic possesses the advanced resources of a major medical center. The testing and treatment capabilities patients will find at Central Plains Clinic range from diagnostic imaging to physical therapy, giving them the trust, confidence, and support needed to regain and maintain their health.

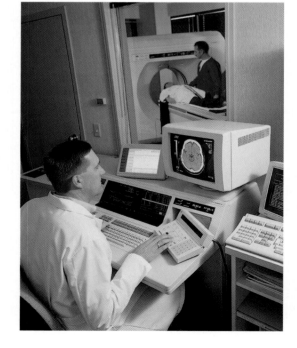

With advanced technology on site, patients receive the highest degree of care possible.

Central Plains Clinic
Exceptional Primary and Specialty Care

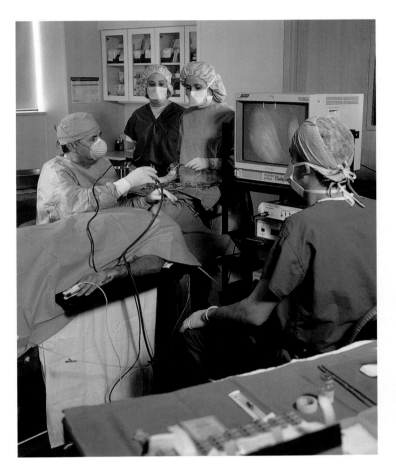

HISTORY

Founded in 1949 by three practicing surgeons and an internist, Central Plains Clinic has evolved over five decades from its original concept to include a blend of talents of many area physicians. It was evident early on that patients appreciated being able to receive many medical services in one facility during a single visit.

With three Doctors Donahoe—Robert R., John W., and S. A.—in addition to Dr. G. I. W. Cottam as founders, the professional association was initially known as the Donahoe Clinic. Following physical expansion at several different sites, in 1976 the name was changed to Central Plains Clinic to better reflect the area served and the clinic's mission.

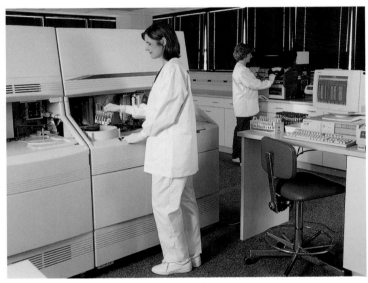

ABOVE: *The Surgery and Diagnostic Center at the main location of Central Plains Clinic is considered to be the most progressive same-day surgical center in the region.* RIGHT: *Central Plains Clinic maintains complete laboratory and testing services on-site to maximize efficiency and ensure accuracy.*

CENTRAL PLAINS CLINIC LOCATIONS

Central Plains Clinic Main
1100 East 21st Street
Sioux Falls, South Dakota
(605) 335-2727 or
(800) 759-4272

Central Plains Clinic Pulmonary Medicine
1201 S. Euclid Avenue,
Suite 407
Sioux Falls, South Dakota
(605) 331-3464

Central Plains Clinic East/ Acute Care
4405 East 26th Street
Sioux Falls, South Dakota
(605) 331-3320

Central Plains Clinic Oncology/Hematology
1000 East 21st Street,
Suite 2000
Sioux Falls, South Dakota
(605) 331-3160

Central Plains Clinic West/ Acute Care
2701 South Kiwanis Avenue
Sioux Falls, South Dakota
(605) 331-3340

Central Plains Clinic Beresford
600 West Cedar Street &
Highway 46
Beresford, South Dakota
(605) 763-5002

United with Central Plains Clinic

Brown Clinic Watertown
506 First Avenue S. E.
Watertown, South Dakota
(605) 886-8482

Medical Arts Clinic Acute Care–Rapid City
717 St. Francis Street
Rapid City, South Dakota
(605) 342-2880

TEAM OF MEDICAL PROFESSIONALS

At Central Plains Clinic there are nearly 110 physicians in more than 40 specialties, which provides the highest level of care to patients. In addition Central Plains Clinic provides convenient acute care services for those patients who are in need of after-hours care in Sioux Falls and the regional centers in Watertown and Rapid City.

Central Plains Clinic is the largest multispecialty clinic in the upper Midwest and the physicians and staff are committed to providing the highest quality, personalized health care services.

AVERA HEALTH

The name Avera Health is relatively new in South Dakota, yet this health system represents a century of service to the people of the state.

At the beginning of the twentieth century, Catholic Sisters established most of South Dakota's first hospitals. Responding to the requests of community leaders, Sisters cared for the sick in Aberdeen, Milbank, Mitchell, Parkston, Pierre, Sioux Falls, Tyndall, and Yankton—and, at one time, in Huron, Rapid City, and Watertown.

By the end of the twentieth century, the two largest communities of Catholic Sisters—the Presentations of Aberdeen and the Benedictines of Yankton—had brought together their scattered single facilities into one system, Avera Health. In 1998 they took the further step of adding the Avera name to the already well-known names of their hospitals, nursing homes, clinics, and other health services. They also offered the option of using the Avera name to their affiliates—community-owned hospitals and physician practices managed by the Sister-sponsored institutions. In all, the Avera name was adopted by more than 100 health facilities in eastern South Dakota and surrounding states.

The dramatic use of one family name, Avera, for so many individual institutions signals a change in thinking about how health care needs

At a special ceremony, a canvas cover billows in the wind and falls away to reveal the addition of the Avera name to the name of a partner hospital. Avera partners at locations throughout the region celebrated the name changes in September 1998.

of South Dakotans can best be met. Working together with their partners in Avera Health, the Sisters hope to accomplish several goals.

One important goal is to strengthen health care in rural areas. Although their own institutions are in the larger cities of the state, the Sisters recognize the necessity of keeping essential health services close to the homes of people in rural areas. In the 1980s they responded generously to requests for help from the trustees of institutions in small towns by providing management services, sharing group purchasing contracts, and helping to recruit physicians. In the early 1990s they developed telemedicine connections. More recently, the small-town affiliates adopted the same measures and standards of clinical quality used by the larger hospitals and nursing homes.

ONE NAME, ONE INTEGRATED SERVICE

The Avera name now communicates to the public that a local Avera health care facility is backed by the extensive resources of the largest health system in the region, including access to specialty care and commitment to clinical excellence.

Catholic Sisters were among the earliest settlers in South Dakota. These idealistic young missionaries from Ireland, Switzerland, and other countries established most of the state's first hospitals and schools of nursing.

The Sisters also hope that people will associate the Avera name with a complete and coordinated continuum of health services, which are organized around people's needs and include prevention and wellness services (the name Avera means "to be well"). The efforts of the Sisters to create an integrated system were recognized twice in 1999 by researchers who independently ranked Avera Health with the top-100 "most integrated" and "most wired" health systems in the nation.

A third reason for using one family name is to let people know that Avera facilities share common values. At a moment in history when religious vocations have declined, and when health care often seems more a business than a ministry, the Sisters want to preserve the essentials of Gospel-motivated care of the sick and elderly. With people of all denominations, they share a desire to assure that life's most profound moments—births, deaths, and physical illnesses—can be experienced in a setting that recognizes God's presence, the innate dignity of human beings made in the image of God, and the promise of life everlasting. The Avera Health ministry is ecumenical, serving the health needs of all, and provides training and support for pastoral care professionals and parish nurses of all religious traditions.

Avera Health's helicopters and fixed-wing aircraft speed patients from the region's rural areas to trauma and specialty centers in the larger cities.

Avera Health partners share a belief that every person is made in the image and likeness of God and must be treated accordingly. Avera provides ministry education for employees, trustees, and physicians; sponsors health ethics conferences; and supports parish nurse programs for people of all religious traditions.

As a new century begins, Avera Health promises in its mission and vision statements to continue "providing quality services guided by Christian values" and to "improve the health care of the people we serve through a regionally integrated network of persons and institutions." To accomplish these goals, the partners of Avera Health—the Presentation Sisters, the Benedictine Sisters, the trustees of community institutions, and many area physicians—will work with many new partners, including schools, social services, churches, government agencies, and other agencies and institutions, to address larger issues that can affect health, such as unemployment, the environment, and public safety.

In so doing, they will build on the tremendous contributions of Catholic Sisters to health care in South Dakota, bringing the mission and ministry of the pioneer Sisters into the twenty-first century.

BELOW: *The cross on the Avera Health logo symbolizes the Christian heritage and mission of Avera partners. The design elements beneath the cross can be interpreted as hands, open and lifted up as in prayer, or as doves, a Christian symbol of peace and hope. Both the design and its color, a deep green, are intended to convey hope and renewal.*

PLASTIC SURGERY ASSOCIATES OF SOUTH DAKOTA, LTD.

THE BOARD-CERTIFIED

PLASTIC AND

RECONSTRUCTIVE

SURGEONS AT

PLASTIC SURGERY

ASSOCIATES OF

SOUTH DAKOTA, LTD.,

IN SIOUX FALLS AND

DAKOTA DUNES HAVE

NUMEROUS "FIRST

IN SOUTH DAKOTA"

ACHIEVEMENTS IN

IMPROVING THE

APPEARANCE OF

THE HUMAN BODY

Plastic Surgery Associates of South Dakota, Ltd., was founded in 1984 by David J. Witzke, M.D., F.A.C.S., and Vaughn H. Meyer, M.D., F.A.C.S., board-certified plastic and reconstructive surgeons. In 1996 they were joined by L. Patrick Miller, M.D. Their main facility is located in Sioux Falls, with an additional fully staffed clinic in Dakota Dunes, as well as outreach clinics in other communities.

The surgeons at Plastic Surgery Associates have completed rigorous plastic and reconstructive surgery training and examination leading to board certification by the American Board of Plastic Surgery and membership in the American Society of Plastic and Reconstructive Surgeons. Doctors Witzke and Meyer also are board certified in general surgery and are members of the American College of Surgeons, open only to those meeting its high professional standards.

The doctors have achieved a number of significant South Dakota firsts:
- First microvascular free tissue transfer,
- First microvascular esophageal reconstruction using the small intestine,
- First to perform microvascular hand reimplantation,
- First to perform craniofacial advancement surgery for congenital craniosynostosis, and
- First to perform liposuction, including the first tumescent liposuction and ultrasonic-assisted liposuction.

The doctors offer a full spectrum of plastic

Plastic Surgery Associates physicians include, from left, Vaughn H. Meyer, M.D., F.A.C.S.; L. Patrick Miller, M.D.; and David J. Witzke, M.D., F.A.C.S.

Plastic Surgery Associates of South Dakota, Ltd.'s main facility is in Sioux Falls, with an additional fully staffed clinic in Dakota Dunes and outreach clinics in other communities.

and reconstructive surgery, including aesthetic procedures such as face lift, breast augmentation, breast lift, ultrasonic liposuction, laser eyelid surgery, laser skin resurfacing, nose surgery, and ear surgery. Reconstructive surgery is available for breast reconstruction; breast reduction; congenital defects; skin, head, and neck cancer; cleft lip and palate; facial fractures; and burns.

Doctors Witzke and Meyer were founders of the first and only burn unit in South Dakota, located at Avera McKennan Hospital in Sioux Falls. Dr. Witzke serves as the director of the unit and Dr. Meyer is the assistant director.

Fully equipped operating facilities are provided in the Plastic Surgery Associates clinics in Sioux Falls and Dakota Dunes to handle office surgery in a confidential atmosphere. Each clinic is staffed with trained professionals who handle patient care in a friendly and caring manner. The doctors are on staff at all Sioux Falls hospitals, the Siouxland Surgery Center in Dakota Dunes, and various other hospitals in the area.

The term "plastic surgery" is derived from the Greek word *plastikos,* which means to mold or change form. The experience and superior training of Doctors Witzke, Meyer, and Miller provide the Midwest with many options for improving the function and overall appearance of the human body.

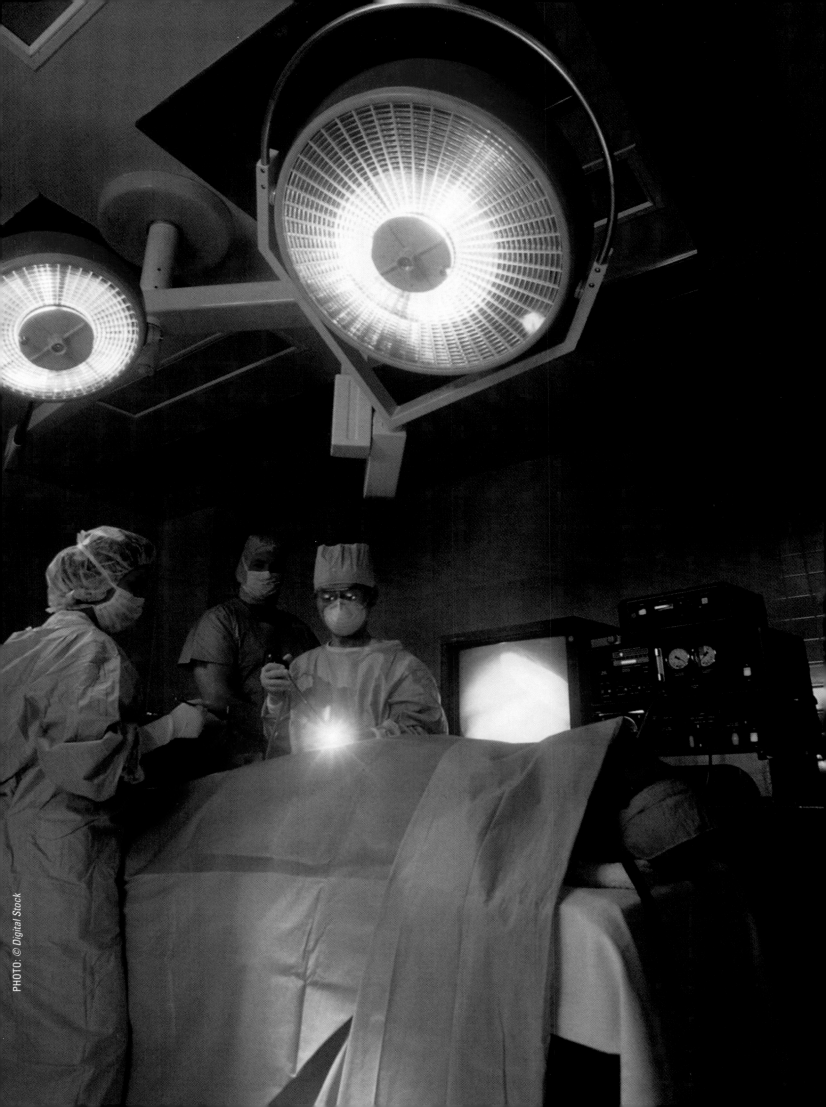

CHAPTER THIRTEEN

LOCATION, LOCATION, LOCATION

Thanks to a combination of factors—a highly favorable business climate; a well-educated and, despite extremely low unemployment, well-motivated workforce; an aggressive, progressive attitude toward high technology; and a concerted effort at both the state and local levels to get the word out about all of the above—South Dakota has been enjoying a boom in development and construction the likes of which have never been seen before.

In the larger communities of the state, construction of homes, apartments, and offices proceeds without pause. Some small, more remote communities have shrunk as a result of the trend toward fewer-but-larger farms, but those closer to South Dakota's larger cities are enjoying a carryover effect from the growth of their bigger neighbors. The population of South Dakota's largest city, Sioux Falls, topped 100,000 in the early 1990s, and is expected to exceed 120,000 by the end of the century. At the other end of the state, Rapid City, although only half the size of Sioux Falls, has seen its population jump from just over 46,000 in the 1980s to almost 60,000 at the end of the 1990s, during which period the state's population increased by nearly 50,000.

IF YOU BUILD IT…

So it is only natural that the Mount Rushmore State is an active contributor to the Midwest's monthly average of 300,000 to 400,000 housing starts. In the first quarter of 1999, Midwest housing starts were up 11 percent over the same quarter in 1998, a year in which new-home sales were up a whopping 17 percent. Locally, in most communities, homes and apartments are going up in record

numbers: South Dakota ranks in the top half of the nation for new housing permits, with about 3,700 in 1998.

Rising almost as fast as the buildings are their valuations. In Sioux Falls, where home prices are generally higher than in other parts of the state, the average home price has gone from about $68,000 at the beginning of the 1990s to almost $112,000 at the end of the decade. But despite the building boom, housing in South Dakota remains affordable. Cost of living comparisons show Sioux Falls with a housing index of 90.3, lower than that of Minneapolis, Des Moines, or Grand Forks. And proactive programs through the South Dakota Housing Authority work to ensure that the American dream of home ownership remains within reach of the average South Dakotan. Indeed, South Dakota stands eighth in the nation for home ownership, with almost 73 percent of residents as kings and queens of their own castles. (The national average is not quite 65 percent.)

At the same time, there is a renewed interest in reclaiming and restoring older homes—"older" around

A new neighborhood takes shape at the southern outskirts of Sioux Falls. The city's population has grown 20 percent in the last 10 years.

PHOTO: © Eric R. Berndt/Midwestock

these parts meaning 80, 90, or possibly 100 years old. The larger communities have established historic districts. The smaller communities, which generally have been in less of a hurry to replace "outdated" structures with something new and shiny, have reaped an unexpected benefit in terms of people who don't mind a 30- or 40-minute commute to jobs in Rapid City or Sioux Falls. (Until very recently "commute" was a virtually meaningless word in South Dakota. Even today, even in Sioux Falls, it is possible to leave the house 15 minutes before an appointment and still have time to grab a drive-through espresso en route.)

In fact, these smaller communities often don't have enough older homes to go around. Most people who grew up in small towns just don't want to leave. Many young families would like to move to small towns, attracted by things like smaller school classes and caring neighbors,

South Dakota's city planners and developers keep architects such as this one busy—and happy—by enlisting their expertise in planning projects to make their communities not just bigger, but better.

STAKING A CLAIM

Beginning in 1863 the Homestead Act granted men and women the right to claim 160 acres (one-quarter square mile) of Dakota Territory land for $1.25 per acre. The claimant was expected to improve the plot with a dwelling and grow crops. After five years, if the original homesteader was still there, the land became his or her property, free and clear. These hardy individuals were known as "sodbusters" because they often had to build their homes from strips of sod for lack of other materials.

but they can't afford to build a new house. To encourage a new generation of South Dakotans to put down roots in these communities, Governor Janklow has spearheaded a unique program. Prison inmates build wheelchair-accessible, two-bedroom bungalows, which older or disabled South Dakotans can buy at cost. The elderly can then sell their larger estates to families that want the extra rooms and big backyards. As of this writing, the state had sold 407 of the bungalows. An added benefit built into this program is that it gives convicts valuable construction skills they can use to join in on the South Dakota building boom when they get out of prison.

SEEING WHAT DEVELOPS

Trying to stay ahead of this explosion of populations, and the explosion of jobs that engendered it, are development departments and organizations in virtually every community. Among the more aggressive have been the Sioux Falls Development Foundation and the Spearfish Economic Development Corporation. The latter was founded in 1980 out of a concern over jobs lost following a fire at the Homestake Sawmill. Since then it has been working with the city's Common Council to attract business and industry to the area, particularly to its light industrial/professional businesses park, anchored by PG Technology, a manufacturer of high-tech construction materials, and O.E.M. Worldwide, which designs and assembles printed circuit boards. Although a small community of fewer than 10,000, Spearfish has been extremely proactive in drawing new and expanding businesses to the Black Hills.

The newly opened Washington Pavilion of Arts and Science in downtown Sioux Falls was converted from an old high school into state-of-the-art performance spaces, galleries, offices, and more.

In southeastern South Dakota, the Sioux Falls Development Foundation has played a key role in that city's incredible but orderly growth. Beginning with the Sioux Empire Development Park in 1970, the Development Foundation has aggressively attracted business and industry to the community, including the high-profile Citibank. Today there are five Sioux Empire Development Parks, and another half a dozen or so in the area. No wonder Sioux Falls is considered one of 10 "Next Big Growth Markets" by *BUILDER Online*.

HOME SWEET HOME

Growing communities are seeing a concomitant boom in residential building, with new developments in the environs of Rapid City, Sioux Falls, and other burgeoning towns springing up as fast as infrastructure providers can keep up. In addition to a prosperity-sparked trend toward bigger, more expensive houses in the range of $200,000 to $300,000 or more—virtually unheard of here only a decade ago—there is a growing interest in building "new old" houses. In Tallgrass Village, a Brandon development, homes are built closer to the street and to each other than in conventional suburban tracts. The houses feature front porches and back alleys, not unlike traditional pre-World War II neighborhoods. Developers and homeowners expect this fashion to head off "urban sprawl" before it gets here, and ensure that South Dakota communities remain close-knit and friendly.

GROWING A FUTURE

Expansion and development is a wonderful and exciting thing, but it generates new challenges. Traffic management, zoning clashes, and basic infrastructural needs such as plumbing and wiring—things rarely a source of concern 10 or 20 years ago—now command much attention at city planning sessions, board meetings, and coffee klatches. The challenges will not abate in the coming century, but neither will South Dakotans' determination to meet those challenges in the exciting growth years to come.

HENRY CARLSON COMPANY

With eight decades in the South Dakota construction industry, Henry Carlson Company has been a leader with a reputation for building high-quality, successful projects in both private and government/public sectors.

Construction projects range from medical to financial, from hospitality to high-tech, from schools to air bases, from libraries to courthouses. The company provides a full range of attractive, functional, and economical construction projects in a wide variety of sizes, shapes, characters, and costs.

HISTORY

Henry Carlson Sr., a 1902 émigré to the United States, began as a construction laborer and subsequently became a skilled stonemason. With William A. Snitkey, Carlson in 1919 formed the Carlson-Snitkey Construction Company. In 1924 Carlson bought out his partner and the company was given its present name—75 years under a single banner.

By the 1930s, the Carlson Company was one of the largest building and construction companies in South Dakota. Under the tutelage of the senior Carlson, the company was responsible for such landmarks as Columbus College (later to become part of the Veteran's Administration Hospital) in Sioux Falls; the Alex Johnson Hotel, in Rapid City; and the State Capitol Annex, in Pierre.

The Henry Carlson Company continues its tradition of involvement in the construction of some of South Dakota's major landmarks on both sides of the state. Shown above is a project the firm built 70 years ago, now a western South Dakota landmark—the Alex Johnson Hotel in Rapid City.

Henry Carlson Company has provided more than 30 years of various construction services for this major midwestern medical facility, the Sioux Valley Hospital in Sioux Falls.

Henry Jr., from the second generation of Carlsons, joined as a laborer in 1943 and, after World War II service, returned to the company in 1950. When the senior Carlson died in 1961 his son was named president. The second-generation Carlson oversaw construction of such South Dakota landmarks as Sioux Falls Arena, Airport Terminal Building, Ramkota Inn, Minnehaha County Courthouse, National Bank of South Dakota, Sioux Falls Public Safety building, and the South Dakota State University Library.

A third generation Carlson, Henry "Chip" III joined the company as an apprentice carpenter in the late 1970s. After earning a college degree in construction, the younger Carlson in 1982 became part of the company's management team.

EVIDENCE OF SUCCESS

Recognizing that the projects it builds are "brick and mortar" examples of Henry Carlson Company success, the company proudly chronicles its most recent achievements: Hutchinson Technology, Sioux Falls; Gateway 2000 renovation and addition, Sioux Falls; Minnehaha County Courthouse addition, Sioux Falls; Animal Disease Lab/SDSU, Brookings; High School/Community Center, Yankton; Mickelson Middle School, Brookings; Medical Building 3, parking ramp, Sioux Falls; Citibank Daycare Center, Sioux Falls;

A new landmark was established in eastern South Dakota with the Minnehaha County Courthouse in Sioux Falls. The Henry Carlson Company created the original building in the 1960s and also constructed an addition in 1996.

as well as a wide range of renovations and additions to religious, educational, and manufacturing buildings in the tristate area.

The Henry Carlson Company is today one of the largest commercial construction employers in South Dakota, southwest Minnesota, and northwest Iowa. The company is committed to providing quality commercial, institutional, and industrial buildings competitively with on-time performance.

This family-operated business has maintained the high-quality work ethic and reputation achieved since the roots of the current operation were planted in 1924. Although Henry Carlson Company has grown exponentially since the early 1920s, personal attention has remained. To manage and supervise its myriad projects, Carlson provides project estimators/project managers as well as field superintendents. This cadre of construction specialists is available for designing, estimating, scheduling, project management, and on-site supervision. The company provides professional, knowledgeable advice and counsel to clients, small and large. These services include the selection of materials and subcontractors that meet client requirements for cost effectiveness and high quality.

AFFILIATED COMPANIES

The Henry Carlson Company owns Asphalt Surfacing Company (ASCO), a paving and road construction company in Sioux Falls. In addition, Kyburz-Carlson Construction Company is the predominant construction firm in the Aberdeen region, providing a wide range of construction services to the public, industrial, and commercial/retail establishments.

Contact Henry Carlson Company, General Contractors, at 1105 West Russell, Sioux Falls, South Dakota 57104, for more information.

Offering the best in planning, technical expertise, scheduling, and cost control, Henry Carlson Company delivers high-quality construction services.

RONNING COMPANIES

PROVIDES ITS

CUSTOMERS—

FROM HOME BUYERS

TO NATIONAL

FRANCHISES—

WITH TOP-QUALITY

CONSTRUCTION AND

SUBSTANTIAL VALUE

In the late 1800s Thomas C. Marson—the great-grandfather of Harriet Ronning, wife of Ronning Enterprises founder D. Wayne Ronning—began building in Sioux Falls, then called the Dakota Territory. LEFT: Marson built the Bishop O'Gorman house, circa 1898. BELOW: Union National Bank, circa 1898, was another Marson project. Courtesy Slate Ronning

The roots of Ronning Companies trace back to the late 1800s when T. C. Marson, Slate Ronning's great-great-grandfather, immigrated from Wales to Sioux Falls in the Dakota Territory and began building his career. Marson, who was the first building inspector of Sioux Falls, built such historic landmarks as All Saints School and Children's Home, as well as numerous houses and structures of quartzite, now listed as Historic Buildings in the National Register.

CONTINUING THE TRADITION

The name Ronning was first used for the company when D. Wayne Ronning, who married T. C. Marson's great-granddaughter, founded Ronning Enterprises in 1956. Its objective: Build affordable, single-family homes for the first-time home buyer. The company's role remained essentially the same, as the post–World War II housing boom fostered affordable home building in west Sioux Falls and later across the city. Ronning worked closely with Federal Housing Assistance programs and subsequently expanded his

company's construction services to building entire subdivisions of single-family residences. To fill the needs of the community, it became necessary to use prebuilt wall panels and trusses to expedite construction. The company's innovative services enabled it to meet the rapidly growing need for high-quality affordable housing.

EXPANDING ON A VALUE

By the 1970s Ronning had expanded its business to include small apartment complexes in Sioux Falls and locations throughout South Dakota and Iowa. Because of this expansion, Ronning Property Management was formed.

The growth of the company's construction and property management businesses led Slate Ronning, D. Wayne Ronning's son, to establish

Ronning Commercial Construction for the purpose of apartment, office building, and retail center construction.

Today Ronning Homes buys land for residential development and builds and sells houses. Its commitment is to compete in the marketplace while giving home buyers the best possible value. Conversely Ronning Commercial Construction develops, builds, and manages commercial properties, including apartment buildings, office buildings, and retail centers.

BUILDING ON A CENTURY OF EXPERIENCE

After more than 100 years of building and construction in the South Dakota area, Ronning Companies can count among its

The Pines at Four Hills Apartments are exclusive luxury apartments that form the focal point of the Four Hills planned development. This Ronning development also includes the Four Hills Townhomes, Four Hills Plaza Retail Center, Four Hills Sinclair Convenience Store, the Harriet L. J. Ronning Library, Norwest Bank, Laurel Oaks Water Park, and Avera McKennan Wellness Center and provides easy access to bicycle trails.

credits the construction of quartzite buildings that now are historically significant, many single-family homes, apartment buildings, offices, and retail centers.

Ronning Companies provides its customers—from home buyers to apartment tenants—with a century of experience and a tradition of top-quality construction and substantial value.

For its second 100 years, Ronning is committed to building, owning, and managing its resources in ways that create value and increase benefits for any community in which it works.

In this construction project at the prestigious Four Hills Ronning development in southeast Sioux Falls, roof trusses illustrate the strength and precision engineering that are an integral part of any Ronning building project.

THE DUNHAM COMPANY

PROVIDING

HIGH-QUALITY SERVICE,

THE DUNHAM COMPANY

HANDLES RESIDENTIAL

AND COMMERCIAL

REAL ESTATE,

PROPERTY MANAGEMENT,

NEW CONSTRUCTION,

AND LAND DEVELOPMENT

IN SIOUX FALLS

AND THROUGHOUT

SOUTH DAKOTA

The Dunham Company's management team provides a strong foundation for a solid company.

Vision . . . it is what Donald A. Dunham Jr. was born with and what has made him a successful developer today. Even as a child on a farm in Union County, South Dakota, Dunham always had the desire, the need, the expectation to learn, to do, and to create more.

In 1977 Don Dunham followed his vision and founded The Dunham Company in Sioux Falls. As the firm's president and CEO, Dunham has created one of the premier full-service real estate and development companies in South Dakota. It handles residential and commercial real estate and property management, as well as property development and construction.

The Dunham Company's motto is Creating Successful Solutions for South Dakota. In living up to its motto, the firm has earned a reputation throughout the state for its financial strength, community leadership, continued customer service, association with

Donald A. Dunham Jr., who founded The Dunham Company in 1977, serves as the firm's president and CEO.

high-quality suppliers, and superior construction work.

"To me, good people are the key to the success of any business operation," says Dunham, who truly believes the single greatest contributor to the company's success is also its most important asset: people.

The citizens of Sioux Falls and all of South Dakota associate the Dunham name with a wide range of projects. Business people credit Dunham with revitalizing downtown Sioux Falls with the construction of new office buildings and a new hotel and restaurant on the Big Sioux River, along with refurbishing many historical buildings downtown. Community activists are aware that Dunham was responsible for the development of Homestead Trails, a residential housing complex for families who might otherwise not be able to realize the ownership of their homes.

A hallmark of Dunham's leadership in its industry is the level of quality in construction management services that the company provides through Dunham Consulting and Construction Services (DCCS). DCCS has completed the construction of numerous apartment complexes, hotels, restaurants, and office buildings.

DCCS also has helped to meet the needs of the state's changing agricultural face, and has emerged as a leader in the construction of livestock complexes.

Dunham Homes is a well-known major player in South Dakota's new home construction market, offering midprice, single-family housing. Providing high-quality construction and more than 20 years of experience, Dunham Homes has

been instrumental in completing a host of developments in Sioux Falls and ultimately expanding to other South Dakota communities, including Elk Point, Yankton, Watertown, and Dakota Dunes.

The Dunham Company is a leader in all facets of real estate: commercial and residential property, sales and leasing, and investment sales. The company provides clients with all the data necessary for them to make sound real estate decisions.

Dunham Property Management, a major facet of The Dunham Company's business, provides professional administrative and accounting services and trained maintenance personnel, paying careful attention to details. The company manages more than 750 residential units plus more than one million square feet of commercial real estate.

Phillips Centre, one of The Dunham Company's many projects, was constructed in 1995 in downtown Sioux Falls. The Dunham Company provided land acquisition, development, construction, investor procurement, and commercial leasing services for the project and continues to manage the property today for the owners.

Serving South Dakota Since 1977

In 1997 Dunham Property Management was expanded to include the management of three Sioux Falls hotels: Country Inn & Suites, Sleep Inn, and Hospitality Inn & Suites.

In describing his vision for the future of The Dunham Company, Don Dunham says, "Our people understand that high quality and service compose the backbone upon which our company has been built. We will continue to provide this quality and service to our customers . . . success is inevitable."

HEGG COMPANIES, INC.

Founded in 1945 in Mitchell, South Dakota, Hegg Companies, Inc., today provides service locally as well as nationally. The unique services that are offered by Hegg include commercial brokerage, property management, hospitality management, and real estate development. There are specialists for each area, in order to better serve customers.

Now headquartered in Sioux Falls, South Dakota, Hegg Companies was founded by Realtor P. Ode Hegg, who sold farmland in eastern South Dakota. The firm now is managed by members of the Hegg family—Peter Hegg, chairman of the board; Paul Hegg, vice president and chief operating officer; and Kristen Hegg Zueger, one of the leading brokers in the commercial real estate sales and leasing division. Throughout more than half a century under Hegg family leadership, the company

Hegg Companies of Sioux Falls, South Dakota, is a property management, development, and commercial brokerage firm with more than 50 years of experience.

Management, development, leasing, and sales of quality properties and businesses.

has demonstrated its expertise in handling projects of all scopes and sizes as well as its background and experience in succeeding in today's highly competitive real estate environment.

The Hegg Companies mission statement spells out Hegg's role in South Dakota's economic life:

"We are the recognized leader in the management, development, leasing, and sales of high-quality properties and businesses in Sioux Falls and the region.

"We are committed to our customers and will exceed their expectations and provide professional service in an ethical manner.

"We are committed to our employees and will provide leadership, cultivate teamwork, create growth opportunities, and recognize outstanding performers."

Hegg's commercial brokerage division provides expert service for individuals or companies involved in buying or leasing office or retail space;

Members of the Hegg family heading up Hegg Companies today include, from left, Paul Hegg, vice president and chief operating officer; Peter Hegg, chairman of the board; and Kristen Hegg Zueger, leading commercial real estate sales and leasing agent.

industrial, manufacturing, or warehouse facilities; commercial investment property; and land for residential or commercial development. Hegg brokers are among the most highly qualified in the nation, with results that testify to the company's top performance on behalf of local and national clients.

The company's property management division manages office, retail, and multifamily properties throughout the entire region. Services of the division include leasing, marketing, renovation, tenant relations, mechanical maintenance, and administrative operations. A major facet of Hegg's property management is for Days Inn hotels in Iowa, Utah, and South Dakota. Peter Hegg, who serves as a member of the Days Inn board of directors, has traveled to China, the Philippines, and South Africa to help open franchises in these countries. Days Inn has been ranked by *Franchise Times* magazine as the twentieth-best (among the top 200) franchises in the nation. In addition to hotel and lodging properties, Hegg manages residential complexes, such as Deer Run Condominiums, and professional facilities, such as the Willow Creek professional building, both in Sioux Falls.

In the ever-increasing field of hospitality management, Hegg is a pioneer and a business leader in today's marketplace. Company professionals provide a complete line of business services, including marketing and positioning, operations management, human resources, accounting and financial reporting, franchise relationships, refinancing and restructuring, conversions and takeovers, design and renovation, recommendations and projections, and project development. Customers of Hegg Companies hospitality management include such commercial giants as Radisson Encore Inn, T. G. I. Friday's, and Days Inn. The services of Hegg hospitality management are individually designed to suit the specific needs of each property—but with the benefit of knowledge and experience gained from years of working with similar situations.

Hegg Companies has developed many projects across South Dakota and the nation, including Deer Run Condominiums in Sioux Falls.

The track record of Hegg real estate development provides ample evidence of prudent, conservative management and close attention to detail. This division provides a full range of services: feasibility studies, site selection, contract administration, construction administration, government permits, and financing. Hegg has developed such major operations as the Midwest Capital Corporation building in Dakota Dunes; the Spiegel Customer Service Center as well as Memorial Park Apartments, both in Rapid City; Ampride convenience stores and gasoline stations in Kansas and other midwestern areas; and T. G. I. Friday's in South Dakota, Nebraska, and Wisconsin.

Hegg's affiliated companies include Hegg Realtors, Inc., one of the oldest residential real estate firms in South Dakota; Northwest Equipment, Inc., of Spencer, Iowa, a John Deere dealership; Dakota Land & Cattle Co., in Gregory and Parker, South Dakota, a grain and cattle operation; and Venture Ranch Inc., of Gregory, South Dakota, a commercial hunting operation.

For the twenty-first century, Hegg continues to look for new ways to use technology to better serve its clients. In addition, Hegg will continue its ongoing search for entities that provide profitability as well as tax benefits for partners who own Hegg-developed or Hegg-managed properties.

Hegg is proud of its more than 50-year tradition of integrity, reliability, and performance and the trust it receives from its customers.

Hegg Companies developed and now manages the Radisson Encore Inn in Sioux Falls, South Dakota.

PARKER GAMING AND ENTERTAINMENT

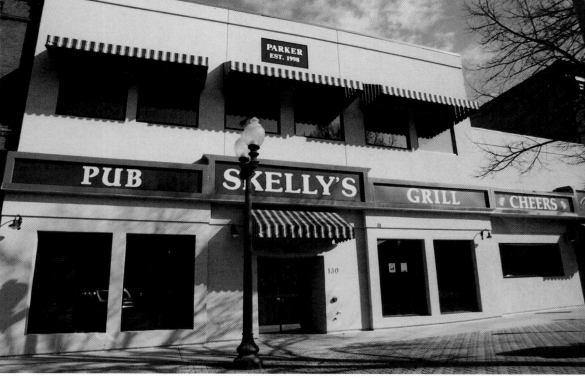

With the special experience of more than a quarter of a century in gaming and entertainment management, John T. Parker Jr.'s firm Parker Gaming and Entertainment is one of the most diversified and interesting companies in the state of South Dakota.

Operating in locations around the nation, the South Dakota–based company offers a single source for the development, management, and operation of successful hotels and casinos. In addition, through its Entertainment Division, the company serves as a talent buyer and booking agency for its customers. Unique to Parker Gaming is the company's specialization in coordinating long- and short-term financing packages for construction and equipment purchases as well as expert architectural design and technical engineering tailored to the special needs of hotel and casino development projects.

John T. Parker Jr. is president and CEO of Parker Gaming and Entertainment.

Skelly's Pub and Grill, located in downtown Sioux Falls, is owned and operated by Parker Gaming and Entertainment. Skelly's is an entertaining Irish-style pub with a complete menu and is known for serving "the best prime rib" in the city.

Parker Gaming advises and counsels about regulatory compliance. The company's legal department is always available to provide clients with knowledgeable expert advice about the establishment and operation of hotels and casinos. When a project is completed, the company is poised to provide expert training for the unique skills required by hotel and casino employees.

Parker's Gaming Division is based on Parker's more than a quarter century of experience serving as general manager, including the supervision of 125 to 2,000 employees, in hotel and casino operations located in Las Vegas, Nevada; Tucson, Arizona; Norfolk, Nebraska; Pickstown and Watertown, South Dakota; and Tama and Marquette, Iowa. Parker is a manager who understands the special talents required to operate small-to-midsize casinos that cater to a local market.

A VARIETY OF COMPANIES

Parker Gaming's roots in South Dakota extend to additional businesses. The company is owner and operator of Skelly's Pub & Grill, located in downtown Sioux Falls. Skelly's is an entertaining Irish-style pub that includes a complete menu and is also known for "the best prime rib" in the city. Parker Gaming also owns the Bergland Center, a building providing classrooms and office space for the Sioux Falls' Center of Public Higher Education (which features educational opportunities that are offered by DSU, SDSU, and USD), and owns or is developing additional rental and commercial office space in the Sioux Falls area as well as casino development countrywide.

New-construction projects by Stencil Corporation include this Lewis Drug and Jubilee Foods' store complex in Brandon, South Dakota. The project was completed in 1998.

PARKER-STENCIL, INC., GETS INVOLVED WITH THE CITY'S PROGRESS

In 1998 John Parker and his partner Clint Stencil combined their years of experience in construction, property development, land procurement, management, and casino development in order to concentrate together on commercial properties in the Sioux Falls area. The two partners are building office, retail, and other commercial projects in the area. Under the corporate title Parker-Stencil, Inc., the organization is providing facility planning, financing, design, construction, property management, and maintenance to a growing list of customers and investors, such as Getty Midwest Title, United States Treasury Department, and Farm Credit Service Bureau. Their construction and property development experience has made them leaders in the community.

STENCIL CONSTRUCTION LEADS IN DESIGN/BUILD CONCEPTS

Founded in 1979, Stencil Corporation is a leader in the design/build concept that enables clients—for commercial offices, manufacturing plants, warehouses, industrial, municipal, agribusinesses, apartments, or updates and renovations—to recognize from the outset of planning the appearance of their project, its construction progress, and cost control through all phases.

Stencil Construction's design/build management and team approach offers advantages that include: implementing client expectations (ensuring that the project meets the client's best interests); single-source responsibility (one contractor for the entire design/build process); hands-on involvement (the direct involvement of Stencil from beginning to end); open-book approach (keeping the client apprised of all project aspects, including costs); dedicated and professional services (a team of professionals continually available); competitive price assurance (relationships with area contractors, which ensures competitive bids for all major aspects of projects); project completion (the design/build team ensures that every aspect of the project is completed before it is turned over to the client)—all coupled with experience in program management and proven performance by a local team.

Evidence of Stencil Corporation's construction successes is visible throughout South Dakota and adjoining states.

Stencil's cooperative ventures under the Parker-Stencil banner provide ample evidence of Stencil skills in construction, construction management, feasibility analysis, property management, finance, ownership ability, lease-backs, and many other services.

Clint Stencil is president of Stencil Corporation, a company with a long line of construction successes.

BABINSKI PROPERTIES

Only in America. It's a time-honored cliché and even the title of a book, but the saga of Don Babinski is living proof that America can indeed be a land of opportunity.

Son of a Polish immigrant who was a builder, Donald S. Babinski began his apprenticeship at age seven, working for his father in Minneapolis. The young Babinski was painting, tearing down old barns (and saving the lumber for future jobs)—as he says, "starting where my father left off."

Self taught, Babinski attended trade school after high school but spent hours in libraries and asking questions of builders in his desire to learn more about the path on which his father had set him.

More than 24 years ago, Babinski moved his base of operations to Sioux Falls, South Dakota, building his first 24-unit apartment complex. Babinski says he chose Sioux Falls because it's a nice, friendly town. "I first discovered Sioux Falls when I drove through with a friend on a hunting trip."

From that first Babinski development came the purchase of 80 acres of land on which he built a series of

Donald S. Babinski is founder of Babinski Properties and founder and president of Dee Bee Management-Leasing, Inc.

In response to a need for large, reasonably priced housing in Sioux Falls, Babinski Properties developed many residential properties, including the Holly 100 apartments on Holly Street, built in 1992. This 106-unit complex was designed to offer "a taste of country in the heart of the city."

apartment buildings. Recognizing that Sioux Falls needed large, reasonably priced housing, he has built such area landmarks as Holly 100, Lakeside, The Sands, At the Lake Townhouses, Englewood Estates I and II, Shadowlawn Terrace, Dawn Lake, NBC Village, and Holiday Manor. Babinski Properties has operations in other states, including Minnesota and Florida. All properties are managed under Dee Bee Management-Leasing, Inc., which was founded by Donald. S. Babinski in 1993.

One of Babinski's dreams for the immediate future is apartment modules that can be constructed in a factory, then shipped and stacked on site to accommodate local conditions and requirements. As Babinski notes, "This modular construction can bring housing to smaller communities, keeping rural towns alive."

Not wanting to stray too far from his roots, Babinski still pounds nails and drives semitrailers loaded with building materials across the country. Moreover, he recognizes the benefits of owning a company in a pleasant area such as Sioux Falls. "It's kind of nice to own buildings in a nice environment," Babinski says.

BAUMGARTNER'S ELECTRIC

THE THIRD

GENERATION OF

BAUMGARTNER'S

ELECTRIC IS

PARTICULARLY PROUD

OF ITS REPUTATION

FOR QUALITY WORK,

ITS STRONG WORK ETHIC,

AND ITS ABILITY

TO TAKE ADVANTAGE

OF TECHNOLOGICAL

ADVANCES

It all began in 1914 in the frontier town of Sioux Falls when James Pryde started Pryde Electric, whose principal business was motor repair and electrical contracting. Pryde's brother-in-law, Al Baumgartner, worked for Pryde before and after serving in World War I. Baumgartner then relocated to Rapid City to start Baumgartner's Electric Company. In 1952 the Rapid City and Sioux Falls firms were combined under the name Baumgartner's Electric. Al's son, Tom Baumgartner, managed the Sioux Falls division from 1952 to 1956, at which time Tom and his wife, Grace Baumgartner, purchased that portion of the company. Both Tom and Grace worked for the company from 1956 until their retirement in 1989. Today Tom's son, Gary Baumgartner, who began working with the company in 1972 as an apprentice electrician, is the company president.

Baumgartner's Electric handles a wide spectrum of electrical contracting, from restoration and updating of historic sites, such as Falls Center and St. Joseph's Cathedral, to modern structures, such as Washington and Roosevelt High Schools, Southeast Vocational Institute, the IBM building, the Western Surety building, Graco manufacturing, Radisson Encore Inn and Convention Center, and a Novus Discover Card processing center. When restoring or updating projects, today's employees often are adapting electrical wiring that Baumgartner's Electric installed 40 to 50 years before.

ⴳ BAUMGARTNER'S ELECTRIC, INC.

When the 50,000-plus-square-foot Jewett Brothers and Jewett Wholesale Foods warehouse, built in 1899, was fully renovated in the mid-1990s, Baumgartner's replaced all the existing electrical systems. The building now houses businesses such as Koch Hazard Baltzer Ltd. Architects and The Sioux Falls Brewing Company. © Jeffery J. Veire

Although wiring continues to play an important role in today's electrical installations, advanced technology, such as high-efficiency lighting, fiber optics, and data-transmission cabling for computer systems, is taking Baumgartner's into the twenty-first century. As Gary Baumgartner notes, "These innovations make it possible for us to improve electrical systems, saving customers money and giving them improved quality." For example, Baumgartner's Electric's exterior relighting project for St. Joseph's Cathedral not only makes the building visible from anywhere in the city, but also cut power consumption by 70 percent.

With nearly 30 electrical professionals on staff, Baumgartner's can handle installations from underground to overhead, from data cabling to high-voltage wiring.

The third generation of employees at Baumgartner's Electric is particularly proud of its reputation for quality, its strong work ethic, and its ability to take advantage of technological advances. The company's long-term relationships with numerous business owners and general contractors is a hallmark of the Baumgartner name.

The new Washington High School in Sioux Falls, which replaced the original school built in the late 1800s, first opened its doors to students in 1992. Baumgartner's work for the 256,000-square-foot facility included all electrical wiring; fire alarm, intercom, and clock systems; data cabling; and the auditorium's stage lighting and sound system. © Stephen Parezo

CHAPTER FOURTEEN

SERVICES THAT SUCCEED

In 1980 Citibank, the credit card processing arm of New York financial behemoth Citigroup, expanded to Sioux Falls, the result of a concerted effort by state leaders to make South Dakota alluring to large financial organizations. A right-to-work state with no corporate income tax, no personal income tax, and a motivated and hardworking labor force, the Mount Rushmore State already had a reputation for being friendly to business.

It then set out to become downright convivial, raising usury rate caps, offering attractive tax incentives to new and expanding businesses, and playing up its favorable bank and financial corporation excise tax.

Now, almost 20 years later, Citibank South Dakota is Sioux Falls' second largest employer, with 3,200 people on the payroll, putting it at the forefront of the state's finance industry.

South Dakota today enjoys a reputation as a center for many types of financial undertakings. Citibank was quickly joined by others, including Green Tree Financial Corporation, a finance company based in Minneapolis, which expanded to Rapid City in 1995 and is now that city's fifth largest employer. SPS Payment Systems, Inc., an Illinois-based credit card processing company, has a Sioux Falls call center, whose activities include handling private-label cards, credit cards that carry the imprint of an organization such as a long distance telephone company or retail concern. These companies and others are constantly expanding, creating more high-paying, high-prestige jobs while further enhancing the state's financial reputation. Already more than 10,000 South Dakotans work in the industry, which generates more than $3.8 billion a year in sales or receipts.

YOU CAN BANK ON IT

Banking enjoys a hospitable home in South Dakota. Major regional banks have long histories here, with branches in most communities. Wells Fargo & Company (Norwest Bank South Dakota, N. A.), U.S. Bank, First National Bank in Sioux Falls, Bankwest, and Marquette Bank are all significant players on the state's banking field.

Growth has not been limited to the big regional or interstate organizations, though. Recent years have seen a proliferation of smaller local banks, with new names such as Deerfield, CorTrust, and First Premier joining such familiar ones as Valley Bank, Rushmore Bank and Trust, and American State Bank. This trend alone says a lot about the state's favorable financial climate.

ARE WE COVERED?

The insurance industry similarly benefits from this boom, and from most South Dakotans' conservative

Consultants from NorthWestern Public Service confer at a job site. NorthWestern is a division of NorthWestern Corporation, whose operations include providing communications and data services, as well as energy-related products, to customers across the country.

habits: According to the U.S. government's 1992 economic census, insurance sales or receipts in the state exceed $1.4 billion a year. Many national companies have a presence here, including Equitable, Prudential, Mutual of Omaha, New York Life, State Farm, and so on. And there are dozens of smaller, often independent agencies in all corners of the state. Health care providers have begun to enter the picture, with Avera Health—a regional assemblage of locally owned hospitals, clinics, and long-term care facilities—offering its own insurance to supplement Medicare.

South Dakota is also the home of nationally renowned Midland National Life Insurance Company. The firm began in 1906, making it one of the longest-lived insurance companies extant. Today Midland

Dain Rauscher's Private Client Group advises individuals on stocks and other financial products. Shown here is the Sioux Falls office.

National has more than $65 billion of life insurance coverage in force in 48 states.

Another homegrown powerhouse is Western Surety Company. Founded in 1900, the firm writes small

GREEN-BACKED

Green Tree Financial Corporation is the nation's largest servicer of government-backed manufactured-housing loans. In 1998 its loan servicing portfolio passed the $30 billion mark.

fidelity and surety bonds, as well as errors and omissions insurance, and has more than one million bonds in force today, more than any other company in the United States. Western Surety's prominence demonstrates that the 5,400 South Dakotans in the insurance industry are well versed in specialized applications as well as more traditional lines.

SEEKING PROFESSIONAL HELP

As the business side of South Dakota's economy has sky-rocketed, it has taken business and professional services along for the ride. Taken as a whole, business services represents one of the fastest-growing industries, with a projected increase in workers of some 44.2 percent between 1996 and 2006. Among the more exciting "growth fields" in professional services are law, accounting, architecture, and consulting.

LAYING DOWN THE LAW

The legal profession has enjoyed substantial growth in the Mount Rushmore State, mirroring a nationwide trend. Today Sioux Falls and Rapid City list scores of lawyers and law firms. Even the smallest communities have at least a couple on hand; and the trend is for law offices in larger communities to open satellite branches in nearby smaller towns.

The state's only law school, the South Dakota School of Law, is at the University of South Dakota in Vermillion. The law school was established in 1901, just 12 years after statehood. About 220 students move

Citibank's presence in Sioux Falls has helped foster a boom in the state's financial services industry. It has also benefited the community by sponsoring resources such as the Citibank Family Center, which offers full-time day care services to company employees.

through the facility in an average year, most of whom graduate to practice in South Dakota.

NUMBER CRUNCHING

As the booming business economy has contributed to an increase in the number of lawyers in the state, so too has it fueled growth in the number of accountants, especially certified public accountants. Sioux Falls is home to 100 accountants and accounting firms. Rapid City has almost as many. Even little Lemmon has three.

Accounting offices range from the traditional one-person shop to big national players such as McGladrey and Pullen, LLP, which has offices in Rapid City, Pierre, and Sioux Falls. Well-known regional firms include the Sioux Falls–based Eide Bailly LLP; LaFollette, Jansa, Brandt and Company, LLP; and Fait Reiter CPAs. In Rapid City, Ketel Thorstenson and Company and Campbell Robinson Burkart Sage are well respected, as is Pierre's Stulken Petersen. These firms, and the others across the state, reflect the increasingly diverse smorgasbord of services that "accounting" represents: bookkeeping and tax preparation, of course; but also business valuation, estate planning, financial planning and consulting, employee benefit setup and administration, data processing, public offerings, and even telecommunications.

EXPERT OPINIONS

Even as accounting firms have begun to wear the hats of financial consultants, data processing consultants, and general business consultants, so too has the number of more narrowly focused consultants increased. There are business consultants Williamson Management Group in Sioux Falls and Midwest Business Services in Rapid City; human resources consultants Benefit Solutions in Sioux Falls; and management consultants such as Kellar Training Associates in Sioux Falls, Frankenfeld

Associates in Rapid City, and Mortenson Consulting in Pierre. That gives you just the barest idea of how big the pool of consultants is, and how much it is apt to grow in the future.

Along those lines, South Dakota's many advertising agencies increasingly position themselves as advertising or media consultants. Paulsen Marketing Communications and Lawrence and Schiller in Sioux Falls and Hot Pink Inc./Franklin and Associates in Rapid City are among the most well-established local firms, having in fact broken out of "local" constraints and become full-fledged regional firms. Also important are the Sioux Falls firms of Henkin Schulz; Media One Advertising/Marketing; Nichols Media Consultants; Bowden Productions; and Echols Communications. In Rapid City, Simpson Advertising, TRI-AD Advertising, and Capture Concepts are to be reckoned with.

These firms and others are not only generating award-winning advertising and marketing materials that stand up against anything produced in bigger markets, they are also, as mentioned, taking on the role of marketing or media consultant, forming important partnerships with their clients that help ensure success for client and agency alike.

BUILDING BOOM

With all this growth, the question becomes, "Where do we put it all?" That's where architects come in. South Dakota's business boom has in turn sparked a building boom, particularly in the population centers. In addition, a fairly new desire to preserve older and historic buildings has generated an increasing demand for renovation services in those communities. On both scores, the state's architectural firms—four dozen or so in number—find plenty of work to keep them busy.

Among the state's better-known firms are Architecture Incorporated; Koch Hazard Baltzer; Holman and Associates; and the venerable Spitznagel Inc. in Sioux Falls. Rapid City's Galyardt Associates and Lund Associates are key players, as is Aberdeen's Herges Kirchgasler Geisler.

CUSTOMER SERVICE

The SPS Payment Systems, Inc., call center in Sioux Falls is open around the clock, fielding questions from holders of SPS clients' private-label credit cards—as well as from callers placing merchandise orders from several catalog companies represented by SPS. The company employs more than 1,000 people in South Dakota and is Sioux Falls' tenth largest employer.

independent agents of all stripes—and also creates opportunities for the state's many credit unions, fraternal insurance agencies (such as Lutheran Brotherhood), and other enterprises both traditional and alternative.

Success breeds success, and as the new century dawns, the story of South Dakota's multifaceted finance, insurance, and professional services sectors is exactly that: a success story.

BELOW: *Marketing experts such as these act as media consultants to help businesses build a national and global presence.*

Renovation projects such as the Washington Pavilion in Sioux Falls, which is also experiencing a general building boom, Rapid City, Spearfish, and elsewhere make this an exciting time for architects in the Mount Rushmore State.

INTO THE FUTURE

South Dakota's professional services industries all seem poised for ongoing growth and profitability in the new millennium. They have seen steady increases in the number of workers since the early 1990s, with no letup in sight.

In finance, the line between "finance" and "banking" or "banking" and "insurance" is becoming ever more thin and elusive. Banks sell insurance and offer brokerage services; insurers provide investment opportunities; brokerage firms offer checking accounts; and so on. Even Gateway is in the game via its Gateway Financial Services. Such diversity opens the field to numerous smaller players—mortgage brokers, financial consultants,

FACING PAGE: *South Dakota attorneys have upheld the law in Belle Fourche's Butte County Courthouse since the early 1900s.*

STAYING COMPETITIVE

Part of South Dakota's friendly business climate includes a well-trained, skilled workforce, and to make sure that remains so, the Governor's Office of Economic Development oversees the South Dakota Workforce Development Program. Businesses and educational institutions work together to coordinate education and training to meet changing needs for new skills, updated skills, and retraining.

SIOUX FALLS AREA CHAMBER OF COMMERCE

THE SIOUX FALLS

AREA CHAMBER

OF COMMERCE

CONTINUES TO

BUILD ON THE VISION,

COMMITMENT,

AND TRADITIONAL

VALUES OF

THE SETTLERS

WHO FOUNDED

THE CITY

At the turn of the twentieth century, some 10,000 settlers who possessed a strong work ethic, a vision for the future, a commitment to family, and a plan to build a better place for future generations, called Sioux Falls their home.

Now the city stands at the dawn of a new century and a new millennium. Sioux Falls is appreciative of those early settlers who helped set into motion the commerce, prosperity, and quality of life that continues today.

Sioux Falls is a city of the future, retaining the positive values of the past. The Sioux Falls Area Chamber of Commerce supports those values. In 2000 the chamber enters its ninety-fourth year. The chamber actively supports the area's business climate. Important community development issues are also addressed as the chamber promotes the economic health and quality of life of the region.

Companies of all sizes find opportunities in Sioux Falls. The largest city and metropolitan area of one of the most business-friendly states in the nation, Sioux Falls has attracted entrepreneurs of varying backgrounds and interests. A number of the city's homegrown operations have become regional, national, and global leaders in their fields. Assisted by a low cost of living, a supportive

Sioux Falls, settled in 1856, is South Dakota's largest city with a population of more than 120,000 people. © Dave Eggen

tax structure, and a highly-productive workforce, Sioux Falls provides the ideal location in which to run a business. With no corporate income, business inventory, and personal income taxes, businesses are attracted to the city and region. Agribusiness also plays an important role along with other major employers in the financial services, technology, retail, and medical/health care sectors.

Traditional midwestern values foster life in Sioux Falls. A robust economy, affordable housing, premium-quality health care, and the warmest hospitality around are all factors in Sioux Falls' growing national acclaim.

The Sioux Falls Area Chamber of Commerce continually strives to build on the early pioneers' vision of the future. With so much to offer as it enters the next millennium, Sioux Falls demonstrates the spirit of its forefathers by continuing to build a better place for future generations.

The site of the Falls of the Big Sioux River, the city's birthplace and namesake, is the most photographed and visited historic site in Sioux Falls. The great natural and scenic beauty of the cascades is complemented by a beautiful park setting. At night, the Falls are beautifully illuminated by high-intensity spotlights. © Rich Naser

FINANCIAL SERVICES >>

THE FIRST NATIONAL BANK IN SIOUX FALLS

THE FIRST

NATIONAL BANK

IN SIOUX FALLS

OFFERS LONG-

STANDING STRENGTH,

STABILITY, AND

TRUST IN BANKING

TO THE BUSINESSES

AND INDIVIDUALS OF

SOUTH DAKOTA

In July 1885 a stalwart group of South Dakotans met with a clear, simple objective—to form a local bank to promote the growth and welfare of Sioux Falls and Minnehaha County. More than 100 years later, that same objective—and commitment—prevail.

Focusing on the individual needs of the citizenry and the unique requirements of the Sioux Falls community, The First National Bank in Sioux Falls has engendered a heritage of strength, stability, and trust. Few financial institutions know local Sioux Falls banking needs better than First National.

In today's era of major bank mergers and long-distance bank ownership, First National Bank takes pride in its local ownership and management. The bank specializes in long-term, service-driven relationships with individuals and business owners who have made successful lives in Sioux Falls and the surrounding area.

LONG-TERM STRENGTH

Chartered in Sioux Falls as Minnehaha National Bank in September 1885, the institution acquired Citizens National Bank in 1888 and Union National Bank in 1896.

In 1889 William Lafayette Baker joined the bank. Members of the Baker family today remain active in the bank's management. In 1929 the bank's name was changed to First National Bank & Trust Company and subsequently to its present name, The First National Bank in Sioux Falls.

The path to today's First National Bank was not without difficulties. During the Great Depression years of the 1930s, many banks nationwide failed. First National Bank was one of only two banks in Sioux Falls that continued to operate uninterrupted at a time when people needed to have trust and confidence in their local bankers. First National provided that strength and resolve.

INVESTING FOR GROWTH

The First National Bank grew along with Sioux Falls over the years by providing banking and other economic functions for the area residents. As the city prospered the bank prospered and was then able to reinvest those resources into the community, thereby promoting vitality and growth.

With total assets exceeding $500 million, First National Bank has 12 locations, including eight in Sioux Falls and locations in Baltic, Brandon, Dell Rapids, and Valley Springs, South Dakota. The bank has created competitive investment opportunities and financed thousands of businesses and homes throughout the area. In a 1997 annual report of trust assets by the Office of the Comptroller of the Currency, First National Bank was recognized as having the largest independent trust department in South Dakota.

First National Bank was among the first to bring automated banking to Sioux Falls with the Advantage Network and today it operates the largest ATM network in South Dakota according to the South Dakota Division of Banking. Looking to the future, the bank has introduced Internet-based home banking, new bank card technologies, and innovative commercial banking and cash management.

The First National Bank in Sioux Falls retains its 114-year commitment to be the principal, locally owned, independent community bank in Sioux Falls and the neighboring communities that it serves in southeastern South Dakota.

FACING PAGE: *Ever since 1929, this eagle—which stands at the entrance of the main office of The First National Bank in Sioux Falls—has symbolized the long-term strength, stability, and trust in banking that compose the bank's long-standing heritage.*

EIDE BAILLY LLP

As businesses throughout South Dakota deal with complex challenges, Eide Bailly continues to emphasize one basic theme: service to its clients. With roots that date back to 1917, the professionals at Eide Bailly have helped people throughout the region successfully reach their business and personal goals. "Each new client and each new task we take on deserve our full attention, renewing the challenge to prove ourselves," says Jeff Strand, partner-in-charge of the firm's Sioux Falls office. "And we wouldn't have it any other way—because our clients' success is our business."

As one of the top-25 CPA firms in the nation according to the *Public Accounting Report*'s "Top 100 for 1998," Eide Bailly brings dynamic strength to businesses in the upper Midwest. "We understand that our clients all have different priorities, different goals, which change based on the maturity level of their business and the stage of life they are experiencing," Strand says. "While success means different things to different people, our focus is on what's important to each client."

As one of the top-25 CPA firms in the nation, Eide Bailly serves clients from offices in six states: Aberdeen, Pierre, Sioux Falls, and Watertown, South Dakota; Phoenix, Arizona; Dubuque, Iowa; Minneapolis, Minnesota; Billings, Montana; and Bismarck, Fargo, and Minot, North Dakota.

A WIN-WIN SITUATION

May 1998 marked an important milestone for the firm. Prior to this date, South Dakota was the home to both Eide Helmeke PLLP and Charles Bailly PLLP, two high-quality CPA firms that each had a strong presence in the Midwest marketplace. When merger discussion began, both partner-groups envisioned a dynamic regional firm that would benefit its clients and the people within the two organizations. It made sense for two well-known consulting and accounting firms to

Helping clients reach their business and personal goals is top priority at Eide Bailly.

join forces, offering clients expanded services and industry specialization, providing the region with enhanced resources and a wealth of expertise, and giving partners and staff new opportunities.

QUALITY STAFF, QUALITY SERVICE

"We take great pride in the professionals representing our firm," says Darrell Strivens, partner-in-charge of the firm's Aberdeen office. "Collectively, they bring diverse backgrounds, talents, skills, and expertise to our team. This team has the tools necessary to contribute to the success of our clients."

With the combined talents of its partners and more than 400 staff members, Eide Bailly provides enhanced specialization and consulting services, which are critical today in business. Committed to providing in-depth services, Eide Bailly hires, retains, and trains highly qualified professionals. To accomplish this, management has added two key positions to its administrative resources: a human resources manager and a training manager. In another step to strengthen the quality of its staff, Eide Bailly adopted a culture statement as their foundation for success which is proudly displayed in each office location and strongly supported by management, as is evident by several programs the firm has implemented.

Darold Rath, managing partner of Eide Bailly, says it is the firm's goal to continue to create jobs and new opportunities for its staff, based on client needs. "We also attract exceptional staff from outside our region because of our large size," Rath says. "This directly benefits our clients."

GOING BEYOND THE TRADITIONAL

The professionals at Eide Bailly include not only tax preparers, auditors, and bookkeepers; but Eide Bailly also provides clients with a business adviser who can assist with all aspects of their business. "We want to help our clients succeed in every way we can. This can only be accomplished by working closely with clients and by developing strong, progressive relationships based on trust," Strivens says. "Our professionals can then help turn a client's goals into reality with creative strategies. At the same time, we can help clients discover opportunities now and for the future." Eide Bailly has a strong consulting practice, as well as professionals who provide the traditional accounting, auditing, and tax services demanded by the business world. The firm is dedicated to developing innovative products and services that are responsive to the continually changing needs of its clients.

MAKING A POSITIVE DIFFERENCE

"We want to make a positive difference in our clients' businesses," says Strand. "To do this, we must be familiar with the terminology of a client's industry and understand all aspects of the business." For these reasons, Eide Bailly has developed industry and service teams to give clients in-depth services. "Our professionals continually broaden their knowledge base through client service, professional education, trade associations, and publications," Strand says. "We keep abreast of industry changes so we can put our expertise to work for our clients."

Technology continually adds new dimensions to the way Eide Bailly does business and to the types of services it offers clients.

As industry rules and regulations become more complex, Eide Bailly has developed strong teams of industry specialists to give in-depth services relating to the client's specific industry.

TECHNOLOGY ADDS NEW DIMENSIONS

Technology is continually adding new dimensions to the way Eide Bailly does business and to the types of services it offers. "In addition to technical professional training, our firm provides its staff with extensive training in hardware and software technologies," Strivens says. Because of the important role technology plays in our personal and professional lives, Eide Bailly offers clients a full array of technology services, including hardware and software needs-analysis and selection, implementation, and training via a mobile training laboratory, as well as continued support.

A COMMITMENT TO COMMUNITY

Eide Bailly is proud to be part of South Dakota and, in particular, the Aberdeen, Pierre, Sioux Falls, and Watertown communities. "We think of our clients as friends who, through our combined efforts as individuals and as representatives of businesses, industries, and organizations, help make our region a highly desirable place to live and work," says Strand. The firm actively supports and participates in service, cultural, and religious organizations. "Community involvement is integral to our personnel development," Strand says. "We contribute time, money, and expertise to the community. It is a privilege to be part of the state's progress, and we intend to be a vital partner in its future." Visit the firm's Web site at www.eidebailly.com for more information.

SPS PAYMENT SYSTEMS, INC.

One of four SPS operations centers, the Sioux Falls, South Dakota, facility employs nearly 1,000 full-time and part-time employees.

SPS Payment Systems, Inc., is a leading third-party provider of consumer private-label credit card programs for national and large regional merchants. The company also provides commercial accounts receivable processing and teleservices, such as technical help-desk support. SPS is a subsidiary of Associates First Capital Corporation (The Associates), a leading diversified financial company (NYSE:AFS).

Headquartered in suburban Chicago, Illinois, SPS originally was established, in 1985, as a part of the Sears, Roebuck and Co. group of financial services companies. SPS was spun off from Sears in 1993. SPS and its affiliate, Hurley State Bank, were acquired by The Associates in October 1998.

An Associates Company

SPS established a large operations center in Sioux Falls in 1987. The South Dakota facility also houses Hurley State Bank, a limited-purpose credit card bank through which SPS issues credit to its private-label cardholders.

SPS serves industries that emphasize point-of-sale and customer service operations, providing its services to both regional and national clients. Industry segments served by SPS include specialty catalog and retail, petroleum/

convenience store, office supply, electronics, Internet service providers, utilities, airlines, on-line information, and health care.

The following are the principal businesses of SPS Payment Systems.

- **Consumer Credit Card Services.** Retailers use private-label credit as a marketing tool to boost sales and build customer loyalty. By outsourcing credit operations, retailers can use their assets to better fund their primary businesses. SPS performs a full range of services including funding; opening new accounts; statement and remittance processing; collections; credit-marketing support; and customer service. SPS is the third-largest outsourcer of private-label credit card services in the United States.

- **Commercial Account Processing.** Outsourcing accounts receivable has gained favor with many credit professionals. SPS offers a billing and accounts receivable management system for clients with business customers. Flexible, fee-based services include new-account processing with electronic access to business credit information. SPS systems allow for procedures to be custom-tailored according to client needs, including monthly revolving accounts or invoice-based billing.

- **TeleServices.** Outsourcing call center services is recognized as a means of reducing fixed overhead and adding to a company's operating efficiency. SPS applies customer service skills and advanced call center technology to provide inbound-call customer support solutions. Highly trained SPS service representatives act as extended staff, performing on-line technical help-desk support and catalog order-entry and handling a variety of product, billing, and service inquiries. SPS has achieved Support Center Practices Certification, recognizing its ability to deliver exceptional services.

Currently SPS Payment Systems employs nearly 1,000 full-time and part-time employees from Sioux Falls and the surrounding area. The majority assist callers with a wide range of needs, including opening new credit card accounts, answering account inquiries, and replacing lost or stolen credit cards. Some teleservice representatives answer questions for the South Dakota Department of Tourism; others provide telephone reservations support for South Dakota campgrounds.

Being a good corporate neighbor is a core value of SPS. Its Sioux Falls management and employees support United Way and a number of other national and local charities through fund-raising activities and volunteerism. SPS recently accepted the Friend of Turning Point Award from Turning Point of South Dakota, and each year SPS employees paint the home of a senior citizen during the annual Brush Up Sioux Falls Paint-a-Thon event.

The Sioux Falls operations center is vital to SPS in providing service to its clients' customers. Every employee shares in the company's commitment to high quality, a keystone of SPS operations. As it approaches the twenty-first century, SPS will continue to explore new technologies for better ways to serve the needs of its wide range of clients.

Contact SPS Payment Systems, Inc., headquarters: 2500 Lake Cook Road, Riverwoods, Illinois 60015; operations center: 811 East 10th Street, Sioux Falls, South Dakota 57103; telephone: (605) 336-5660; fax: (605) 336-5781; or visit the SPS Web site at www.spspay.com for additional information.

SPS uses state-of-the-art telecommunications equipment to aid its service representatives in providing exceptional customer service.

For the annual Brush Up Sioux Falls Paint-a-Thon event, a community involvement program, SPS employees volunteer to paint the home of a Sioux Falls senior citizen.

FIRST DAKOTA TITLE

In January 1989 First Dakota Title was founded, with a small office in Sioux Falls. The company's objective was to modernize the title insurance business of South Dakota by using advanced electronic technology to shorten the time needed to conduct title research—a task formerly done by hand. First Dakota Title became the largest title company in the state.

There now are First Dakota Title offices in five counties. Offices in Minnehaha and Lincoln counties serve the Sioux Falls area; the Codington county office serves the Watertown area; and the Union county office and Yankton county office serve the Dakota Dunes area.

Prospective home buyers and current home owners can rest assured that their property title is free of complications when the title insurance policy is written by First Dakota Title.

First Dakota Title offers its customers financial stability, state-of-the-art technology, quality service, and a knowledgeable, accessible staff.

All First Dakota Title offices are located within the state of South Dakota, and the company works with other organizations nationwide to provide premier title insurance and closing settlement services. These partnerships, along with its specialized technological tools, have put First Dakota Title on a par with successful title insurance companies across the United States.

Relying on its technology to store each aspect of title background, First Dakota Title has immediate access to the records that pertain to every real estate transaction that has occurred in the five counties it serves—from records that date back to the original land patents to records of present-day transactions.

As this Dakota-grown company progresses into the twenty-first century, First Dakota Title is committed to ongoing expansion and to continuing to provide the same unparalleled service to its business and individual clients that it has offered for more than a decade of the twentieth century.

HOME FEDERAL SAVINGS BANK

Home Federal Savings Bank's chairman, president, and CEO, Curtis Hage, summarizes the company's current position in the following way: "By virtue of careful planning, foresighted management, and exceptional staff performance, Home Federal Savings Bank (HFSB) has carved its niche as a responsive, service-oriented company committed to its customers, stockholders, and the economic growth of its communities."

The origin of the bank was as a state association formed to help residents of South Dakota with home loans and savings. It was established more than 70 years ago, in March 1929, and called Home Federal. Its services were expanded and the bank continued to evolve. In 1982 it became Home Federal Savings Bank. HFSB is a wholly owned subsidiary of HF Financial Corp. HF Financial Corp. is a publicly held company traded under the symbol HFFC.

In 1983 HFSB entered into a major expansion mode, acquiring several financial institutions in South Dakota. With each acquisition the bank further expanded its markets and broadened its customer base.

Today Home Federal Savings Bank, headquartered in Sioux Falls, where it was founded, concentrates on serving families and businesses in eastern South Dakota. It operates 20 South Dakota branches in 15 communities: Aberdeen, Brandon, Brookings, Canton, Dakota Dunes, Dell Rapids, Freeman, Hartford, Lennox, Mobridge, Parker, Pierre, Redfield, Sioux Falls, and Winner. Its Internet banking serves customers nationwide.

Through its commitment to local South Dakota communities, HFSB adheres to one of its slogans: It starts

Home Federal Savings Bank officers and staff are committed to focusing on the customer.

at Home. It stays at Home. In an era of giant corporate banks and mergers, HFSB finds that its local roots and continuing presence in South Dakota are valued by its customers.

The bank's commitment to customer service includes a full range of financial services, from basic checking accounts to business banking, commercial real estate, investment management, and trust services. The use of advanced technology enhances the bank's ability to offer progressive services such as Internet banking and on-line bill paying from its Web site at www.homefederal.com.

HFSB operates two active, wholly owned subsidiaries: Hometown Investment, Inc., insurance company and Mid-American Appraisal Service.

HFSB moves into the next century with a record of strong growth and a commitment to leading-edge technology, along with full recognition that the longtime business axiom "The best source of new business is existing customers" is the foundation of the success it has built over more than 70 years.

Home Federal Savings Bank, the first South Dakota bank to offer Internet banking and bill-paying services, serves clients via its Web site at www.homefederal.com.

Home Federal
Savings Bank

WELLS FARGO & COMPANY (NORWEST BANK SOUTH DAKOTA, N. A.)

SERVING THE PEOPLE

OF SOUTH DAKOTA

FOR MORE THAN

A CENTURY,

NORWEST BANK

OFFERS PRODUCTS

AND SERVICES

TAILORED TO MEET

THE NEEDS OF

ITS CUSTOMERS

To The Nth Degree®

With a history of more than 110 years in South Dakota, Norwest Bank South Dakota, N. A., truly has become a one-stop financial solutions store, determined to "out national the locals and out local the nationals" with products and services tailored to meet the needs of its customers.

A STRONG FOUNDATION

Founded in 1890 as State Banking and Trust Company of Sioux Falls, Norwest has served the people of South Dakota and has been an integral part of the progress of its communities. In 1914 Norwest was known as Security National Bank of Sioux Falls. In 1929 "Trust Company" was added to the title. In 1935 it became Northwest Security National Bank and in 1984 four of its banks (Aberdeen, Rapid City, Sioux Falls, and Watertown) were consolidated into a single bank, Norwest Bank South Dakota, N. A. Today Norwest serves 32 South Dakota communities through 52 stores. Moreover, Norwest is the only bank in South Dakota with stores located on two Native American reservations.

Through its century-plus history in South Dakota, the bank has been a vital contributor to the community. Areas of charitable giving focus on higher education, youth, United Way, and local and regional initiatives. A few of the education and regional projects include the Norwest Community Scholarship Fund, eighty $1,000 scholarships

Through the HUD 184 Loan Program, Norwest has become a leader in providing private financing options to Native American families and housing authorities who otherwise could not acquire housing loans because of the unique legal status of Native American land.

given to high school seniors who are furthering their education at a South Dakota higher learning institution; the Mount Rushmore Preservation Fund; and the South Dakota Hall of Fame.

A RICH FUTURE

With a vision for meeting its customers' needs where, when, and how they like to bank, Norwest offers extended banking access through services like the Phone Bank℠ 24-hour Center, allowing customers to open accounts, transfer funds, apply for loans, and check account balances any time of day. The bank also offers ATM service and free Online Banking. Norwest is a statewide leader in providing innovative banking products to its personal, business, and agricultural banking customers.

Norwest, which merged with Wells Fargo & Company in 1998, will be known as Wells Fargo & Company in the new millennium, enabling the bank to provide more products and services for its customers. Already active in all 50 states, Canada, the Caribbean, Latin America, and other international financial centers, Wells Fargo will project an even stronger presence worldwide. Norwest—under its current banner and, in 2000, under the Wells Fargo name—will continue to be committed to its customers and communities.

LEFT: Mount Rushmore Memorial superintendent Dan Wenk helped dedicate the Borglum Court, honoring the memorial's sculptor, on July 30, 1998. Norwest contributed more than $250,000 to this portion of the Mount Rushmore Preservation Fund restoration efforts. RIGHT: Norwest provided financial support for the construction of four footbridges on the Mickelson Trail, a 110-mile hiking and biking trail in the Black Hills completed in 1998. Norwest employees volunteered their services for the project.

DACOTAH BANKS, INC.

Rodney Fouberg, CEO and chairman of Dacotah Banks, Inc., parent company of the Dacotah Bank system, summarizes his business philosophy in the following words: "A good company with strong local connections, along with professional, personable employees who pay attention to customers' needs and are accessible, can really deliver the best of both worlds: high-tech and high-touch service." This statement also is a reflection of the way the Aberdeen-headquartered bank operates.

With a presence in South Dakota that goes back more than 100 years, Dacotah Bank now serves more than 40,000 customers at 19 local bank offices in 17 markets. The South Dakota communities that are home to Dacotah Bank include Aberdeen, Bison, Bradley, Clark, Cresbard, Faulkton, Henry, Lemmon, Mobridge, New Effington, Rapid City, Roslyn, Sioux Falls, Sisseton, Watertown, Webster, and Willow Lake.

"The offices are staffed with people with whom you can entrust your money, who listen to your ideas for a new business, who show you how to realize more potential from your farm or ranch," says Fouberg. "They are people who know your name and the names of your children, people you see in church."

ALLIANCE OF FRIENDS

"We spell our bank's name identically to the original Lakota Sioux interpretation," Fouberg explains. "The word

Although the oldest community bank in the Dacotah system dates back to 1897, the present-day operations of Dacotah Bank grew from this small Aberdeen Main Street location, chartered in 1955.

'Dacotah' means an alliance of friends—and we take that seriously around here."

Although retaining its personal, hometown flavor, Dacotah Bank provides its customers with a full range of modern financial and banking technology. Bank customers can use ATMs, ATM CheckCard, Dacotah Visa cards with no annual fee, and 24-hour Dacotah Phone Banking; they also enjoy extended hours at drive-through locations. Embracing today's technology, the bank has its own Web site (www.dacotahbank.com), an interactive site that includes information about the bank's products and services. Customers visiting the Web site can apply for new or additional accounts, conduct secure banking transactions, review their accounts, and even pay bills on-line from home or office.

DOING BUSINESS FACE-TO-FACE

Even with an increasing number of people doing their banking through ATMs, by phone, or over the Internet, Dacotah Bank management at all levels remains committed to doing business face-to-face. They believe firmly that the slogan Dacotah Bank is Here for You is a reflection of the service customers receive every time they do business with Dacotah.

Dacotah Bank's branch in downtown Sioux Falls exemplifies the company's blending of traditional customer convenience and twenty-first-century technology.

INSURANCE >>

AFLAC, INC.

The firm of AFLAC, Inc. (American Family Life Assurance Company), was named the number-one insurer by *Forbes Global Business & Finance* in the magazine's January 1999 ranking of "The World's Best 400 Companies." In the same month *Fortune* magazine included AFLAC as the number-one insurance company (ranked 13th overall) in its annual listing of the "100 Best Companies to Work for in America."

The Columbus, Georgia–based company is a leader in the field of voluntary employee-benefit plans.

AFLAC first began its business activities in South Dakota as the American Family Life Assurance Company more than 30 years ago, in 1968. In 1984 it began operating as AFLAC. Today AFLAC insures more than 40,000 South Dakotans, with more than 68,000 policies in force. More than 2,200 South Dakota businesses make the company's voluntary employee-benefit plans available to their employees. In addition, AFLAC

Members of AFLAC's Dakota coordinator staff, gathered here, work with the 200 licensed AFLAC representatives operating throughout the state.

AFLAC, Inc.'s South Dakota headquarters office is at 1600 4th Street NE, in Watertown, South Dakota.

administers more than 900 Section-125 benefit plans in South Dakota.

AFLAC maintains South Dakota sales and service offices in Sioux Falls, Rapid City, Yankton, and Brookings, as well as in Watertown, where the company's state headquarters office is housed.

Since 1989 Michael J. Tomlinson has been state sales coordinator, responsible for 10 regional and district sales coordinators and 200 licensed AFLAC representatives across the state. AFLAC has operated in South Dakota now for more than 30 years. William J. Meyer began the state operation in 1968.

AFLAC, a Fortune 500 company, is listed on the New York and Tokyo stock exchanges. A. M. Best Company has given AFLAC an A+ (superior) rating; *Standard & Poor's* and Duff & Phelps have awarded the company "AA" ratings in claims-paying ability; and Moody's Investors Service rates AFLAC Aa3 (excellent) for insurance company financial strength.

As one of the largest insurers in South Dakota, AFLAC takes great pride in its more than three decades of service. The company is committed to providing the finest voluntary benefit solutions into the next century.

WELLMARK OF SOUTH DAKOTA, INC.

While health care insurance in the United States predates the Civil War, in South Dakota prepaid health plans date back just slightly more than 50 years. And Wellmark Blue Cross and Blue Shield of South Dakota has led this development from the beginning. In 1948 Blue Cross was started in South Dakota with 35 member hospitals. Then in 1956, with the support of 100 South Dakota physicians, South Dakota Blue Shield began operations. That same year Blue Cross and Blue Shield entered into service contracts that enabled the Blue Cross sales force to sell the Blue Shield medical service plan along with its own hospital plan.

As the delivery of health care in the United States evolved, so did Wellmark's products. In 1986 the first managed care product in South Dakota, AWARE, was offered by Blue Cross and Blue Shield. In 1987 the first electronic claims were transmitted by South Dakota hospitals to Blue Cross.

In 1989 three insurers—Blue Cross of Western Iowa and South Dakota, Blue Cross of Iowa, and Blue Shield of Iowa—merged to form IASD Health Services Corporation, doing business in South Dakota as Blue Cross of South Dakota. South Dakota Blue Shield remained independent.

By the 1990s it became apparent that the requirements for health care service in South Dakota had expanded significantly. In 1996 Blue Cross of South Dakota and South Dakota Blue Shield merged to form a new South Dakota insurance company—South Dakota Health Services Company (SDHS), doing business as Blue Cross Blue Shield of South Dakota.

Wellmark Blue Cross and Blue Shield of South Dakota is the state's largest domestic health insurance company, providing services to more South Dakotans than any other health care insurer. Its product portfolio is designed to meet the needs of all South Dakotans, whether they have a group health care insurance plan or an individual policy.

In 1997, when its parent company became Wellmark, Inc., SDHS changed its name to Wellmark of South Dakota., Inc., doing business as Wellmark Blue Cross and Blue Shield of South Dakota. This name change marked the insurer's first move from being a traditional insurance company to being a health-improvement company with a new mission and focus.

The new name was created to combine the idea of *well*ness for both the individuals and the communities Wellmark serves, and *mark*, short for the benchmark of improving business operating procedures and performance. Wellmark incorporated these ideas into its mission, which focuses on providing a broad array of high-quality, accessible cost-competitive health products and services for the purpose of helping members improve their health.

One of the first health-improvement projects Wellmark undertook was to determine the health status of the residents of South Dakota. The inaugural edition of *The Wellmark Report: Health in South Dakota* was released in the fall of 1998. This was the first such report to profile the health status of the citizens of 42 South Dakota communities. The report shows the following at a glance:

Wellmark Blue Cross and Blue Shield of South Dakota has been providing services to South Dakotans for more than 50 years. During customers' years in the workforce, Wellmark builds relationships with them that carry over into customers' retirement years. More South Dakotans choose Wellmark's Senior Blue Medicare supplement insurance than any other supplemental coverage.

- the state areas where particular diseases most often occur,
- local area variations in the ways health care is provided,
- for each area, comparisons of the local community rate for common diseases and certain medical or preventive procedures to statewide rates and national benchmarks.

Community and state health professionals use information from The Wellmark Report to identify local health improvement opportunities and launch community initiatives.

Wellmark Blue Cross and Blue Shield of South Dakota also is involved in other health-improvement initiatives with the state of South Dakota and serves as a partner in the state's Diabetes Control Project, the Breast and Cervical Cancer Control Program, and the South Dakota Coalition for Adult Immunizations. Wellmark also partners with the Wegner Health Sciences Information Center at the University of South Dakota School of Medicine by sponsoring the Wegner Wellness program, a free consumer health and health-professional information service.

With the South Dakota Department of Health, Wellmark also cosponsored the Caring Program for Children for six years until 1998, when Medicaid was expanded. The Caring Program provided free, primary preventive health care to children whose parents could not pay for private health care coverage yet did not qualify for Medicaid. Wellmark donated staff, materials, and financial support for the program.

Today Wellmark is the largest domestic insurance company in the state of South Dakota providing services to more South Dakotans than any other health care insurer (*A Guide to the Division of Insurance and Comparative Statement*, published by South Dakota Commerce and Regulation,

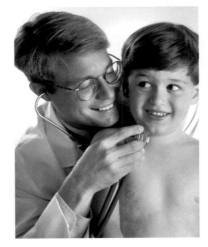

Wellmark Blue Cross and Blue Shield of South Dakota has one of the largest networks of contracted providers in the state, plus a panel of providers worldwide through the Blue Cross and Blue Shield Association's Blue Card program.

In 1997 the company changed its name to Wellmark Blue Cross and Blue Shield of South Dakota. The new name is a combination of wellness and benchmark. This change was the firm's first move from serving as a traditional insurance company to becoming a health-improvement company.

September, 1998). Its large market share can be credited in part to its diverse portfolio of products. Wellmark provides services to meet the needs of all South Dakotans, including those with group insurance and those with individual coverage.

Wellmark employs nearly 200 professionals and contracts with independent agents statewide. The corporate office is located in Sioux Falls, with sales and support staffs located throughout the state. Provider-affairs consultants are located in both Sioux Falls and Rapid City.

Wellmark has adopted a set of values that shape the organization and reflect its commitment to members, communities, staff members, and health care providers. These values are:
- Integrity: Be honest, fair, and forthright, meet obligations.
- Caring: Offer respect, compassion, understanding, and community service.
- Continual learning: Provide an environment to encourage the staff and give employees opportunities to expand skills.
- Empowerment: Bestow staff members with trust and the authority to take risks and make independent judgments.
- Energy: Encourage employees to be customer-driven and to work with vigor, agility, and commitment.
- Continual improvement: Strive to perfect and mature.
- Impeccable service: Meet and exceed the expectations of health care plan members and providers.

For more than 50 years Wellmark Blue Cross and Blue Shield has been the leader in health care insurance in South Dakota. As we enter a new millennium Wellmark will continue to develop programs and services to make South Dakota a healthier place to live and work.

WELLMARK
Blue Cross and Blue Shield of South Dakota
An independent licensee of the Blue Cross and Blue Shield Association

MIDLAND NATIONAL LIFE INSURANCE COMPANY

It has been said that all people, all organizations, all companies can be divided into three classes: those that are immovable, those that are movable, and those that move. Like the people and the state in which it thrives, Midland National moves. From its beginnings in 1906 Midland National has possessed the vision, the integrity, the ingenuity, and the strength to become one of the leading life insurance companies in the nation.

Midland National was born on a late summer evening in the Black Hills of South Dakota. Meeting at the Smead Hotel in Lead, South Dakota, a group of six men— John Walsh, Joseph Moore, Charles Turney, Claude Sterling, Daniel Bannister, and Fred Smith—elected officers for a company to be known initially as Dakota Mutual Life Insurance Company. They decided the company would be founded to serve the life insurance needs of South Dakotans, and its home base would be in Watertown, South Dakota.

Even back then the company had a firm vision for its purpose: to provide an honest policy that gave the people of South Dakota the opportunity to protect their families and to potentially build

ABOVE: *An early photograph depicts Midland National Life's home office, the Granite Block Building, on the southeast corner of Broadway and Kemp Avenue in Watertown, South Dakota. A popcorn wagon is parked in front of the building.*

LEFT: *The company seal features an oak tree, a symbol of the founders' philosophy and slogan, Great Oaks from Little Acorns Grow. This slogan was adopted in 1906.*

up their estates by working with a life insurance provider dedicated to giving value to its policyholders.

Symbolizing the philosophy of its founders, who borrowed $2,500 as their start-up fund, the company's original slogan was Great Oaks from Little Acorns Grow. And grow the company did—both in size and strength. In 1909 it reorganized as a stock company in order to raise capital for its continued growth, dropping "Mutual" from its name in 1915 and changing its name to Midland National Life Insurance Company in 1925.

The company's growth and strength enabled it to endure some of the most challenging times of the twentieth century, including World War II; the influenza outbreak of 1918, which eventually killed between 20 and 30 million people worldwide; and the Great Depression of the 1930s, when Midland National demonstrated its

Many farmers were able to get back on their feet during the economic hardship of the 1930s because of Midland National Life's pig program.

characteristic ingenuity by financing premiums with pigs. The company gave brood sows to farmers on the condition that the farmers would pay the premium on their life insurance policy when they sold the grown pigs. This practice not only kept the company alive but also helped the people of South Dakota survive the hardships of the times.

Making it through both the difficult and prosperous times, Midland National has continued to thrive, expanding to serve policyholders across the nation and in several areas around the world. In 1970 the company recorded its first $1 billion of life insurance in force, and moved its home office from Watertown to Sioux Falls, South Dakota, in 1977. In 1979, upon the official opening of its new home office, Midland National embarked on a period of unprecedented growth, with $10 billion of life insurance in force recorded in 1982, $25 billion in 1989, $50 billion in 1992, and more than $65 billion in 1997.

Great oaks do from little acorns grow, and Midland National owes much of its success to its sound investment philosophy, a broad range of high-quality life insurance products, and its policyholder value. Midland National Life is operated independently under the ownership of Sammons Enterprises of Dallas, Texas, which is one of the largest privately owned companies in the United States.

While its original integrity, ingenuity, and strength continue to define the company today, Midland National habitually recalls the past, examines the present, and prepares for the future, continually seeking new ways to deliver what it calls "Life at its Best." For its employees and agents, "Life at its Best" means excellent benefits, quality service, and support from a top-quality corporate staff. For its policyholders, "Life at its Best" means the best

The facade of the Midland National Life Sioux Falls office building is 22,000 square feet of gold-toned glass, which helps reduce heating and cooling costs, saves fuel, and makes optimum use of daylight illumination.

life insurance products at the best price. With continued product innovation, technological development, strategic alliances, and a mission to be the best in the business, Midland National strives to move and grow, serving policyholders in South Dakota, across the nation, and around the world.

CULBERT DAVIS COMPANY INSURORS

A LARGE

INDEPENDENT AGENCY

BASED IN SIOUX FALLS,

CULBERT DAVIS

COMPANY INSURORS

USES 40 YEARS

OF EXPERIENCE

TO PROVIDE

COMMERCIAL AND

PERSONAL INSURANCE

SERVICES FOR

CUSTOMERS IN THE

FIVE-STATE REGION

Since 1959, Culbert Davis Company Insurors has provided innovative commercial and personal insurance products and services to fit individual customers' needs. Today this large independent insurance agency has achieved the perfect blend of excellent service and professionalism.

Culbert Davis uses a local approach with a global perspective. The agency has formed strategic partnerships with more than 20 of the insurance industry's best companies, delivering cost-effective plans for customers in a variety of industries: manufacturing, construction, wholesalers/distributors, medical, professional, environmental remediation, and many more.

Risk administration programs have been part of the company's product offering since the beginning. The full-time, full-service commercial department designs custom insurance programs including commercial property and liability, workers' compensation, automobile, professional liability, loss control, umbrella and excess liability, boiler and machinery, directors' and officers' liability, product liability, surety and fidelity bonding, and consultation.

Culbert Davis has been providing coverage for employee benefit programs since the agency's first policy was written 40 years ago. Products include employee benefits, life and health, financial planning, annuities, consultation, home, and automobile.

The personal lines department tailors plans for home, auto, and life insurance needs. As families grow, Culbert Davis ensures that proper coverage is always available.

The strength at Culbert Davis Company Insurors lies in the company's experience in researching coverage to meet individual needs. Each policy is

Culbert Davis Company Insurors values the trust its clients place in the company to represent the things people value most: families, homes, and businesses.

a customized program. When a claim is submitted, the full-time dedicated claims department responds immediately. The agency offers the latest claims management practices, loss reviews and controls, and risk management assessments.

At Culbert Davis Company Insurors, offering the best products and service in the industry means hiring and training a dedicated customer service team. The agency provides policy updates and contractual reviews to help customers stay competitive and ensure optimum value in all policies.

As the world changes, Culbert Davis also changes, continuing to increase the company's presence in the national and international markets. Services have been expanded to include growth in the franchise marketing niche, in self insurance, and in domestic and offshore captive companies.

Culbert Davis Company Insurors values the trust its clients place in the company to represent the things people value most: families, homes, and businesses.

Culbert Davis is headquartered in Sioux Falls, serving a client base in the five-state region. The agency is licensed to provide insurance coverage in nearly all 50 states.

Culbert Davis' research capabilities provide the foundation for offering the best insurance, risk management, and surety bonding services in the country.

ENGINEERING AND ARCHITECTURE >>

BANNER ASSOCIATES, INC.

The mission statement of Banner Associates, Inc., is "To provide quality architectural, engineering, land surveying, and related services to our clients in an atmosphere of honesty, creativity, integrity, and professionalism." Founded in 1947 by J. T. (Joe) Banner, the firm has fulfilled this mission, providing broad-based civil engineering services in the Great Plains and Rocky Mountain states for more than 50 years. With steady growth since its inception—evidence of the company's dedication to customer service and sound management—Banner Associates has become one of the region's premier engineering firms. Headquartered in Brookings, South Dakota, Banner also has offices in Grand Junction, Colorado; Laramie, Wyoming; Marshall, Minnesota; and Rapid City, South Dakota.

Banner Associates, Inc., provided architectural, structural, and civil/site design services, as well as construction administration services, for the George S. Mickelson Middle School, completed in 1998 in Brookings, South Dakota. The innovative "HOUSE" concept for teaching and learning was the basis for design.

The company's wide range of expertise includes architecture; civil, structural, and computer engineering; water resource planning and development; transportation and sanitary engineering; construction services; and land surveying.

Clients have included private and public utilities, government agencies, industrial and commercial firms, and private individuals. Banner has provided services for literally thousands of projects—from small, local efforts to complex, multidiscipline programs—in the western United States, especially South Dakota, Minnesota, Wyoming, and Colorado.

ENGINEERING EXPERTISE

With a select team of more than 70 professional engineers, architects, and specialists, the company can appoint broad-based teams tailored to handle the unique challenges presented by a project. Banner carefully matches skills to the needs of each project, to best serve its clients.

The 57th Street Tunnel under I-229 in Sioux Falls, South Dakota, is the longest cut-and-cover tunnel ever constructed in South Dakota. Banner provided civil/site, structural, and electrical design services for this roadway structure, completed in 1998.

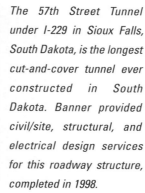

Banner has been an active provider of water resource planning and development services to industries, municipalities, state and federal agencies, and private industry. The company has employed extensive hydrologic and hydraulic capabilities, along with computer modeling, in the development of surface and groundwater supplies and the design and construction of dams, intake structures, pumping plants, and transmission and distribution pipelines. Banner also advises clients on water rights, regulatory permits, and licenses. The firm has constructed dams and reservoirs on a number of challenging geographic sites in South Dakota and Wyoming.

Banner handles all facets of water and wastewater treatment, from planning and design to construction services. The firm provides comprehensive planning and design services for water and wastewater treatment facilities, appurtenant pipe systems, and water storage tanks and towers. Banner also can provide start-up assistance, operator training programs, troubleshooting guidance, remote-controlled data acquisition systems, and operation and maintenance manuals. South Dakota is dotted with water and wastewater facilities designed by Banner.

Banner's transportation engineering expertise includes planning and feasibility studies; roadway, bridge, and airport design; drainage design; and construction engineering and monitoring. The firm's engineers have designed more than 1,500 miles of roadways for interstate, primary, secondary, and urban highway systems. Structural engineers have designed more than 200 major bridges and inspected and analyzed more than 2,500 bridges under the National Bridge Safety Program. Working

Midwinter preparation is conducted for the design of the new Mount Rushmore parking structure entrance and exit roadway system, which is adjacent to the recently completed visitor's center in South Dakota's Black Hills.

with the Federal Aviation Administration and state aeronautic commissions, Banner has provided planning, design, and construction for air traffic facilities in South Dakota and Wyoming.

A major segment of Banner's work is in the area of municipal engineering, where they provide engineering services for water and wastewater systems, parks and recreation facilities, storm-water drainage improvements, and city street improvements. The firm also has been involved in the development of major recreational facilities in such geographically diverse locations as Colorado, Minnesota, South Dakota, and Wyoming.

Other services available from Banner include military engineering, computer engineering, materials testing, land development, surveying, and construction administration.

Banner Associates provided architectural, structural, civil/site, process, and control system design services for the Big Sioux Water Treatment Plant in Egan, South Dakota, and oversaw the construction of this unique softening plant, which was completed in 1994 using a new, innovative technology.

TSP GROUP, INC.

FROM MODEST

BEGINNINGS

AS A SMALL

ARCHITECTURAL OFFICE,

TSP GROUP, INC.,

HAS GROWN INTO

A MULTIFACETED

ORGANIZATION THAT

OFFERS COMPLETE

DESIGN AND

CONSTRUCTION

SERVICES TO A WIDE

RANGE OF CLIENTS

The City Hall in Sioux Falls, completed in 1936, was Harold Spitznagel's first notable project. A newspaper account of the day described the building as "ultra-modern, a masterpiece of beauty and utility."

broad range of design services and capabilities.

Throughout 70 years of operation, the TSP Group has grown significantly, and now has more than 200 employees in ten offices across five states. These firms have a strong local presence, yet are able to use the great breadth and depth of resources available at other TSP Group office locations. A multidiscipline team

Backed by a history of strength and stability, TSP Group has grown from a small architectural firm known as The Spitznagel Partners, established by Harold Spitznagel in Sioux Falls, to a multi-service design and construction organization. Today TSP projects dot cities, towns, and landscapes all across South Dakota. Projects that are a blend of art, science, aesthetics, and functionality grace every major city in the state.

With roots tracing back to 1930, TSP began its expansion in 1969 when it opened an office in Rochester, Minnesota. In 1973 the firm expanded to Rapid City, South Dakota. Subsequently, TSP opened offices in Minneapolis, Minnesota; Denver and Fort Collins, Colorado; Sheridan, Wyoming; and Marshalltown, Iowa. In 1982 TSP added Delpro Corporation, enabling the group of firms to add professional construction services to its already

Harold Spitznagel, renowned architect and founder of TSP Group, is shown here circa 1970.

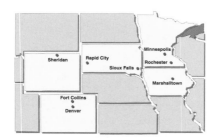

TSP GROUP, INC. AFFILIATED OFFICES

- TSP Group, Inc., Sioux Falls, South Dakota
- Spitznagel, Inc., Sioux Falls, South Dakota
- Delpro Corporation, Sioux Falls and Rapid City, South Dakota, and Minneapolis, Minnesota
- TSP Three, Inc., Rapid City, South Dakota
- TSP One, Inc., Rochester and Minneapolis, Minnesota
- TSP Two, Inc., Sheridan, Wyoming
- TSP Five, Inc., Denver and Fort Collins, Colorado
- TSP Six, Inc., Marshalltown, Iowa

Contact a TSP Group office or visit the group's Web site at www.teamtsp.com for additional information.

of skilled professionals, TSP can meet any design, engineering, or construction challenge. Services include architecture; structural, mechanical, civil, and electrical engineering; landscape architecture; interior design; and construction management, design/build, general contracting, and project management. TSP is ranked in the top-500 design firms in the United States by the prestigious publication *Engineering News Record*.

Looking to the next century, TSP's vision is for expanded services and capabilities to include predesign/feasibility studies and project development services. The group continues to explore geographic expansion in the region. In addition, it is strongly committed to the use of advanced technology to better serve its clients.

TSP is dedicated to making its clients comfortable and confident in doing business with the organization—no matter where the location. With the motto Quality, Service, and Integrity . . . Attitudes to Build On, the TSP family of companies provides its clients with every service necessary to bring an idea to reality. Its philosophy stresses community involvement, personal service, long-term relationships, and the unique approach of . . . listening.

Hamlin Education Center, a TSP project near Hayti, South Dakota, exemplifies a high-quality midwestern educational facility. The center features an NCAA-size state-of-the-art gymnasium complete with cross-courts, bleachers, and an aerobic-sensitive floor. © The Imagery Photography, Sioux Falls, South Dakota.

THE SERVICE INDUSTRY >>

NORTHWESTERN CORPORATION

NorthWestern Corporation, headquartered in Sioux Falls, South Dakota, is recognized as one of America's fastest-growing publicly traded companies. NorthWestern's family of partner entities represents strong leadership positions in customer service and business solutions markets. The company's focus today includes communications and data services, energy, air-conditioning, heating, plumbing, and other related areas. As NorthWestern executes its vision to be "America's Best Service and Solutions Experience," it is committed to reinventing customer service and redefining business solutions for the twenty-first century.

NorthWestern Corporation's family of partner entities represents strong leadership positions in customer service and business solutions markets.

NORTHWESTERN CORPORATION'S FOCUS INCLUDES COMMUNICATIONS AND DATA SERVICES, ENERGY, AIR-CONDITIONING, HEATING, PLUMBING, AND OTHER RELATED AREAS

Today the NorthWestern family includes Blue Dot Services Inc., fast becoming one of America's leading full-service providers of air-conditioning, heating, plumbing, and related services; CornerStone Propane Partners, L.P., America's fourth-largest and one of its fastest-growing publicly held retail propane distributors; Expanets, Inc., one of the nation's premier providers of networked communication solutions to businesses; and NorthWestern Public Service, a provider of competitive, reliable electric and natural gas service and value-added services. Headquartered in Huron, South Dakota, NorthWestern Public Service supplies retail electricity to 108 communities

and natural gas to 57 communities, with a service area spanning 26 counties in the state. Through 7,000 team members, NorthWestern Corporation and partner entities collectively serve more than one million customers across the United States.

Founded in 1923 as NorthWestern Public Service, a provider of electric and natural gas service, NorthWestern has built its success over the past 75 years on attention to customers and innovation. In 1994, anticipating the competitive forces changing the global consumer services industries, NorthWestern began a series of strategic steps to position itself as a leader in the marketplace of tomorrow. Since its repositioning, Northwestern has achieved six years of record-breaking revenues and earnings growth. In 1994 NorthWestern's revenues were $157 million;

Richard R. Hylland, president and COO, and Merle D. Lewis, chairman and CEO, are leading NorthWestern's dynamic growth.

in 1998 annualized revenues reached $2 billion.

Merle D. Lewis, chairman and CEO of NorthWestern, attributes the company's outstanding performance to the enthusiasm, innovation, and hard work of team members. "Our talented men and women build and strengthen customer relationships by delivering quality products, creative solutions, and unprecedented service—24 hours a day, 365 days a year. Backed by a determination to continually reach higher and motivated by the pride that comes with success, they are responsible for the exciting transformation within NorthWestern."

In South Dakota, three entities are teaming together with NorthWestern Public Service to provide a broader array of products and services to Midwestern customers. NorthWestern Services provides an extensive line of residential services including heating, cooling, and value-added products for customers' convenience, safety, and security. Commercial services include energy management, HVAC design, installation and maintenance, lighting design, and more. NorthWestern Energy provides energy packaging and marketing alternatives as well as consultative and management services to large and midsized commercial and industrial energy customers. NorCom Advanced Technologies, Inc., provides a one-stop solution for integration of voice, data, and video telecommunications needs.

Because the key to success is talented, dedicated, and resourceful people, NorthWestern constantly invests in adding specialized skills, as well as cutting-edge technology, to keep pace with a rapidly changing world.

NorthWestern's performance is the result of successfully taking advantage of growth prospects. As the company expands and develops, the diversity of its businesses contributes to more consistent and predictable profitability.

NorthWestern's experienced, knowledgeable professionals help customers maximize their energy investment.

Richard R. Hylland, president and chief operating officer, sees opportunities to grow in every area of the organization. "As substantial as our achievements have been," says Hylland, "we are even more excited about the capabilities and strategies we are putting in place for the next millennium."

More and more businesses look to North-Western to help reduce costs and maximize performance and competitiveness. In response, NorthWestern develops customized solutions that range from applying state-of-the-art communications and technology to addressing a firm's unique energy needs. As NorthWestern continues to strengthen its brands, expand its geographic markets, and develop unlimited opportunities for team members, the company remains intensely committed to providing customers with the right products while setting new standards for service.

NorthWestern carries and installs its own line of heating and air-conditioning products.

CHAPTER FIFTEEN

POWER AND MOTION

South Dakota's central location has long made it vital to transportation. Indians, and later traders and trappers, found this a good place to meet well before the United States united. The covered wagons came through here, then the railroads, then the interstate highways. East/west Interstate 90 and north/south Interstate 29 meet at Sioux Falls, making that city a crossroads in the literal as well as the figurative sense.

KEEP WATCHING THE SKIES

The state is well served by commercial airlines. Northwest, United, and TWA are at home on South Dakota runways, as are commuter airlines such as Mesaba (Northwest Airlink), United Express, and Air Vantage. Charter services such as B&L Aviation in Rapid City, Business Aviation in Sioux Falls, Capital Air Carrier in Pierre, and others, are carving out their niche, delivering packages and passengers. Sioux Falls Regional Airport, the state's busiest, sees 25,000 to 30,000 boardings a month.

The "majors" are also well represented in air freight and package services, with offices in the larger cities: Emery Worldwide, Airborne Express, BAX Global, UPS, DHL Worldwide Express, and Federal Express; plus local companies such as Rushmore Air Freight Service in Rapid City, Package Delivery Company in Sioux Falls, and others.

IT'S OUR CUSTOM

In 1996 a U.S. Customs Port of Entry was established at the Sioux Falls Regional Airport, further underscoring South Dakota's importance in transportation. The Port of Entry benefits not just the air transport industry but trucking and warehousing as well. Clearing customs locally improves the bottom line for several companies, especially UPS, which runs daily cargo flights from Calgary, Canada. The nascent Port of Entry and its five foreign trade zone sites will grow in importance as the world shrinks in the future.

ALL THE LIVE-LONG DAY

The railroad put South Dakota on the map, turning tiny villages such as Aberdeen and Sioux Falls into important rail centers. Though passenger service is no longer available, freight transportation remains vital.

Key figures in South Dakota railroading are Burlington Northern Santa Fe Railroad (BNSF), which operates almost 600 miles of its own track as well as almost 400 owned by the state; and the Dakota, Minnesota and Eastern (DM&E), headquartered in Brookings, which owns almost as many miles as the BNSF, plus operating rights on lines owned by that company and the

Today South Dakota has 4,140 bridges, and both railroad and interstate cross the river at Chamberlain. In 1880 the railroad stopped at Chamberlain, and passengers and freight were ferried across the Missouri River to reach the ranch land and mines to the west.

state. There are several smaller operators, such as the D&I Railroad, which hauls rock, gravel, and grain products from Dell Rapids to Sioux Falls and Sioux City, Iowa; and CP Rail, which hauls farm products and fertilizer between Veblen and Veblen Junction, North Dakota.

It remains to be seen where the rails will lead in the new century. The DM&E has a plan to build nearly 1,000 miles of new railroads and upgrade more than 200 miles of old track to connect Wyoming coal fields to Minnesota shipping centers. If approved, the project will generate an estimated 6,000 construction jobs and 2,000 permanent jobs.

MOVIN' ON

The trucking industry boasts 13,000 companies operating in South Dakota, including major lines such as ABF Freight System in Aberdeen, Rapid City, Sioux Falls, and Watertown; Quast Transfer in Rapid City and Sioux Falls; and Yellow Freight System in Rapid City, Sioux Falls, and Watertown. Heavy-truck drivers are in demand, with that occupation enjoying an annual growth rate of about 11 percent.

Sioux Falls Regional Airport offers connections to more than 200 cities in the United States and many international destinations, plus several daily nonstop flights to Minneapolis–St. Paul, Chicago, and other major midwestern cities.

Coach lines are represented by national carrier Greyhound Bus Lines and locally owned Jack Rabbit Lines. Greyhound generally brings passengers into and out of the state, while Jack Rabbit chauffeurs them within the state's borders. Jack Rabbit also offers charters and tours.

THE SHORT WAY AROUND

South Dakota has 83,358 miles of highways, roads, and streets. A small percentage of that number belongs to Interstate 229, a bypass of Interstate 29 that rings Sioux Falls, making South Dakota's largest city the smallest metropolis in America to have its own interstate highway bypass.

THE POWER OF WATER

Residents of the Mount Rushmore State enjoy some of the least expensive electricity in the United States, ranging from less than three cents to just over eight cents per kilowatt-hour. The value of electricity from hydroelectric plants on the Missouri River is about $160 million per year.

South Dakotans enjoy cheap, reliable electric power, which may be why the state has not rushed to deregulate its electric utility industry. Here, a crew strings high-voltage power lines near Sioux Falls.

PLUGGING IN

Power goes hand in hand with transportation, and South Dakota's utilities in no way lag behind. Rural electrification and the Pick-Sloan plan ensured a dependable, widespread electric supply for the state. Good thing, because statewide demand for current has grown exponentially.

Electricity comes to South Dakota customers via numerous routes: large regional utility companies such as Northern States Power, Black Hills Power and Light, and NorthWestern Public Service; smaller ventures such as Otter Tail Power Company and Montana Dakota Utilities Company; rural cooperatives such as West River Electric Association and Rosebud Electric Coop; and municipal power companies in smaller communities.

THINKING AHEAD

South Dakotans' fondness for technology cuts two ways: The many benefits are indisputable; but technology, and the concomitant growth, may ultimately overtax our reserves. Perhaps reflecting on a time not long ago when water and power were neither widespread nor dependable, the state has begun to lay the groundwork for a utility-supply system that will meet needs and expectations across the Mount Rushmore State well into the new millennium.

Most electricity is generated by the massive turbines at the dams along the Missouri River. Together, the four generating plants produce more than 1.5 million kilowatts in a typical year, enough to meet area needs with some left over to sell.

OTHER POWER PLAYS

As the twentieth century winds down, South Dakota is exploring other energy sources. Eight buildings in downtown Philip are heated geothermally, utilizing the earth's own internal combustion engine. Lake Wagner Greenhouse, also at Philip, and St. Mary's Hospital in Pierre likewise warm space with hot water from within the earth.

The state has a commitment to ethanol, the corn alcohol–based gasoline extender. Research into automobile fuels that contain 50 to 80 percent ethanol—as opposed to the usual 10 percent—is currently underway. If these studies prove favorable, agriculture proponents and researchers will likely turn their attention to other renewable, or "green," energy sources in the form of crops that can be burned to spin turbines or otherwise create power.

THE WETTER THE BETTER

Water is of paramount importance as bigger communities expand and attract new business, industry, and residents. The Missouri dams ended South Dakota's status as a water-poor state, but the statewide pipeline envisioned with the project never materialized. Much of the state is served by wells and aquifers, and there is no immediate supply concern. But several typically forward-thinking South Dakota communities have resurrected the idea of a Missouri River pipeline. These efforts should bear fruit early in the twenty-first century.

NorthWestern Public Service provides electric and natural gas power and value-added services to customers throughout the upper Midwest. Headquartered in Huron, the company supplies retail electricity and maintenance to 108 South Dakota communities.

NORTHERN STATES POWER COMPANY

In South Dakota, North Dakota, Michigan, Minnesota, and Wisconsin, where weather extremes increase demands on the delivery of gas and electricity, nearly 1.4 million residential and business customers have come to rely on Northern States Power Company for their power needs. NSP crews usually are called on several times each year to brave the elements in order to restore service to customers safely and as efficiently as possible.

Through the early efforts of Northern States Power Company (NSP), the rural area near Renner, South Dakota, had electric power as far back as 1923. A few of the families who were provided electricity for the first time on December 23, 1923, gathered here to mark the occasion. Since then, NSP service to rural South Dakota has grown to supply nearly 10,000 customers in 35 communities.

SERVING SOUTH DAKOTA

NSP was established in South Dakota in 1916, the result of a number of mergers and consolidations of electrical lighting and engineering companies. One such firm, the Sioux Falls Electric Light Company, constructed the first hydroelectric plant in the state, on the Big Sioux River in Sioux Falls in 1884. Another firm, the H. M.

NSP's Pathfinder plant, on the Angus C. Anson site just east of Sioux Falls, is used to provide electricity during times of peak customer use. Originally built in 1964 as the Pathfinder Atomic Power Plant for conducting research on nuclear power, the facility was converted in 1968 to one that generates electricity by using natural gas. © Rusten Film Associates

Byllesby Engineering Company, built a 1,500-kilowatt hydroelectric plant in 1908.

With service to the Sioux Falls area firmly established, NSP moved to bring electrical power to rural South Dakota. Customers in the rural area near the town of Renner, South Dakota, were provided with electricity on December 23, 1923. To inaugurate the use of electricity from its newly completed 2,300-volt power line, NSP gave the customers strings of colored lights for their holiday trees. NSP's service to rural South Dakota has since grown to provide electric power for nearly 10,000 customers in 35 communities.

PATHFINDER FOR NUCLEAR POWER

In 1957, having signed a contract with the Atomic Energy Commission for research and development of nuclear power, NSP announced plans for the construction of the Pathfinder Atomic Power Plant on the Big Sioux River east of Sioux Falls. In 1964, after seven years of planning and construction, the plant attained its first sustained nuclear chain reaction. Over the years the plant provided a wealth of knowledge and experience to NSP and the industry; many of NSP's Pathfinder employees went on to become leaders of other successful NSP nuclear power plant projects in Minnesota, at Monticello and Prairie Island.

In 1968, with the Pathfinder research having ended and plans for the new Minnesota plants well under way, NSP began its conversion of the Pathfinder plant to one that produces electricity from natural gas. After a period of nuclear cooldown, NSP became the first investor-owned utility to decommission its own nuclear plant and safely shipped the reactor vessel to a low-level radioactive waste site in Washington state.

In 1993 the site of the Pathfinder plant was renamed the Angus C. Anson site, for the NSP–South Dakota chief

An ice storm that was to besiege the region for eight days hit eastern South Dakota on November 16 in 1996. NSP crews worked around the clock removing ice from power lines and restoring service to customers.

executive who died, along with South Dakota governor Mickelson, in an airplane accident on April 19, 1993. The plant currently is used to produce electricity during times of peak customer use, supplementing the base-load electrical production provided by other power plants. Two 125-megawatt natural gas–fired combustion turbines completed in 1994 also are located on the Angus C. Anson site.

NSP AND THE FUTURE OF SOUTH DAKOTA

NSP has been serving customers in South Dakota for more than 80 years. Throughout that time NSP has maintained a strong partnership with Sioux Falls and all of South Dakota. NSP's industrial customer base has been growing at the rate of 6.5 percent annually for more than a decade. Today Sioux Falls is the third-largest—and the fastest-growing—community that NSP serves in the five-state region.

NSP contributes to the social and economic well-being of its service area through community and economic development efforts, corporate contributions, employee volunteerism, investments in affordable housing, and stewardship of the environment.

As the utility industry evolves, NSP remains dedicated to the continued economic development of South Dakota. NSP will continue to provide reliable, economical energy services to customers in South Dakota for many years to come.

Familiar NSP symbols Reddy Kilowatt and his co-worker Reddy Flame light the way for economic development into the next century.

MIDWEST COAST TRANSPORT

In 1949 in an old tin shack near the stockyards of Sioux Falls, South Dakota, Midwest Coast Transport was founded as a small refrigerated-trucking company. It consisted of four leased trucks for transporting goods for two local clients—John Morrell & Company, a meat purveyor, and Nash Finch, a grocery wholesaler. Because its loads were hauled from the Midwest to the West Coast, the company was named Midwest Coast Transport (MCT).

For 50 years MCT's reputation has been built on reliability, honesty, safety, dedication, and premier service as an irregular-route truckload carrier. Today MCT's fleet of 1,000 trucks transports perishable and general commodities for shippers in 48 states. MCT continues to transport goods for its first two customers. The company's nearly $135 million in 1998 revenues ranks MCT among the top-10 carriers of its type in the United States.

In December 1993 Comcar Industries of Auburndale, Florida, acquired MCT, positioning it as a significant element in a half-billion-dollar transportation system. The merger brought together two transportation giants, giving Comcar additional market presence in the northern United States and giving MCT even greater financial strength and confidence for the future in a burgeoning national transportation system.

Midwest Coast Transport has an independent contractor fleet of 1,000 trucks that transports perishable and general commodities throughout 48 states.

More than 1,200 drivers deliver freight around the nation night and day. Ease of communication between drivers and the supporting staff at MCT terminals ensures on-time delivery whenever the customers request. Drivers use an onboard computer system to communicate with the dispatch office, while satellite tracking automatically and continuously updates the truck's location, so customers can routinely determine the status of their freight. In addition to its three Sioux Falls offices, including headquarters, MCT has facilities in Sanford, Florida, and West Chicago, Illinois, as well as a sales office in Bloomington, Minnesota. From its Florida site, MCT operates one of the largest operations in the United States for consolidating and shipping tropical plants. One example of MCT professionals' careful handling and transporting of a wide range of plants and trees is its shipments for the largest indoor family entertainment park in America—the woodsy, seven-acre Knott's Camp Snoopy, at the Mall of America in Bloomington, Minnesota.

MCT is distinct in having each of its trucks owned and operated by an independent contractor or fleet operator. The MCT logo is on each truck and owners take pride in the quality, appearance, and performance of their equipment. Fleet owners make up more than three-quarters of the MCT tractor fleet; the balance are one-truck owner/drivers. A score of ownerships are second- or third-generation family-owned businesses.

MCT values its drivers and independent contractors and has a driver turnover rate that is far below the industry average. The company works to assure that its customers receive value-added transportation services that meet the customer's expectations. MCT's on-time performance record is regularly acknowledged by customers, who consider MCT a carrier-partner in their businesses.

The safety and reliability of its transportation services is an MCT hallmark. Its drivers' records are among the safest in the nation, with an accident frequency far below the industry average. MCT's safety record has earned the company 23-straight first-place safety awards in its category by the South Dakota Trucking Association. In addition, MCT drivers have been recognized on a national level with such honors as Independent Contractor of the Year and America's Road Team awards.

MCT is extensively involved in safety activities and programs. The company's safety awards program ties incentives to accident-free driving and recognizes drivers' accomplishments. The company sponsors drivers for the South Dakota Trucking Association Driving Championships and its team has earned the trophy for three consecutive years.

MCT's championship drivers earned the South Dakota Trucking Association team trophy for the third consecutive year in 1998.

To keep MCT independent contractors supplied with high-quality drivers, the company has operated a driver training school for more than 25 years. This five-week program encompasses safety skills, defensive driving techniques, equipment care, Department of Transportation regulations, and paperwork processing. In addition, emphasis on customer satisfaction and service are vital elements of the driver education courses. Graduates are placed with experienced drivers who work with them under real-world conditions. Hundreds of MCT-qualified driver-graduates have progressed to become independent contractors, operating their own businesses.

What the next 50 years hold for MCT will be exciting to see, but one constant has carried Midwest Coast Transport for the past half a century and continues on into the future—service. MCT's award-winning fleet of independent contractors continues to outgrow and outperform all expectations, upholding high standards of safety, professionalism, and service. From its humble beginnings, MCT has been recognized as a premier carrier at the state and national level for its safety and reliability. MCT's management people look forward to the challenges of the next 50 years.

While the MCT logo is found on every tractor, each rig is as individual as the contractors who own them.

CHAPTER SIXTEEN

RICHES OF THE LAND

No one would be surprised to learn that agriculture is South Dakota's dominant economic sector, but even some

locals are surprised to learn that livestock, not cash crops, dominates agriculture. Despite the towering stalks of

corn, the amber waves of grain, the seemingly endless fields of soybeans, oats, flaxseed, and sunflowers, some

60 percent of the state's farm economy—about $3 billion a year in cash receipts—is from livestock sales.

"Livestock" encompasses the obvious bovine and porcine constituents, plus poultry (chickens, ducks, and turkeys); sheep and lambs; and even bees: there are more than 100,000 bee colonies here. Cattle are most important. At any given time, between 3.5 and 4.5 million head of cattle are found in South Dakota. Nationwide the state ranks ninth in production of cattle and calves, fifth in beef cows, eighth in cattle on feed, and seventh in calf crop (births).

In some ways the cattle industry is the perfect amalgam of Old West ranching and Midwest farming, since even West River range cattle are shipped to southeastern South Dakota to be fattened. The southeast is where the corn is, and so are most of the stockyards and packing plants. Meatpacking has long been important here, with the John Morrell plant at Sioux Falls among the state's biggest employers. IBP, Cimpl Packing Corporation, and others in Rapid City, Mitchell, Yankton, Huron, and elsewhere, process more than 650,000 cattle a year, as well as sheep, lambs, hogs, and pigs. South Dakota ranks fifth in the nation in sheep and lamb production, and ninth in hog and pig production—sending about three million of these little piggies to market every year.

FEWER BUT BIGGER

Since the early 1900s, the number of farms in South Dakota has been dropping—but the farms have grown larger than ever. South Dakota remains tops not just in livestock but also in crop production, yielding about $1.2 billion in cash receipts per year. Nationally, our farmers find themselves in the top 10 for production of corn, wheat, flaxseed, and sunflower seed; and typically number one for rye and oats. Soybeans, sorghum, hay, and potatoes are important cash crops, too.

Another change since the days of our grandparents and great-grandparents is that farms are now fully electrified, fully mechanized and, increasingly, fully digitized. Today a South Dakota farmer is as likely to be found working a computer mouse as jockeying a combine. Farmers utilize sophisticated weather-tracking computers and real-time market data to plan and execute their work. They also proactively seek new markets for their products as well as new products to market.

Thick forests of pine and spruce make the Black Hills appear black. Two-thirds of the Hills' roughly 6,000 square miles lie in South Dakota, where wood products generate close to $200 million a year.

PHOTO: © Digital Stock

FILL 'ER UP

Chief among new products is ethanol, the blend of gasoline and alcohol distilled from corn. Developed as a fuel-extender in the 1970s, ethanol is now a legitimate product in its own right. The American Coalition for Ethanol recently announced a proposal for a $44 million ethanol plant, the largest in the Dakotas and Minnesota, to be built near Madison. This plant, overseen by Sioux Falls–based Broin and Associates, will be operational by mid-2001.

IT BELONGS TO US

In 1897, President Grover Cleveland set up 13 forest reserves, including the 967,680-acre Black Hills Forest Reserve. Today most of the timberland in the Hills is public land, with the U.S. Forest Service selling logging rights to lumber companies.

The Homestake Mine in Lead is the largest producing gold mine in the Western Hemisphere. Homestake's deepest shaft is 8,000 feet. The mine has been in continuous operation since 1876.

ALL FALL DOWN

Although "South Dakota" may call to mind fields and farmsteads, logging has been a vital industry in the Black Hills since at least the gold rush of 1876. Mining is a lumber-intensive endeavor, and towns tended to spring up around mines. Mine operators and town developers felled 1.5 billion board feet of timber between 1876 and 1898.

Modern conservation philosophy has revamped logging and milling practices, and one of the results has been clever innovations in the use of what was once considered scrap. By-products of Black Hills logging operations today include wood chips sold to paper mills; mulching and landscaping chips; sawdust; and pellets to burn in

A CASE OF GOOD THINKING South Dakota played a key role in United States logging history. The first government-regulated timber cut took place near Nemo in 1899, an event still on the books as *Timber Case No. 1*. Previously, logging on public lands was virtually unregulated. But beginning here, the National Forest Service took a proactive part in preserving public forests.

woodstoves. Often, waste from the milling process is used as fuel to help power the mill.

By-products presuppose product, and in the Hills that means lumber. About 335 million board feet, most of it ponderosa pine, come from the Hills' 1,447,000 acres of timberland every year. South Dakota's lumber industry employs more than 3,000 people, a figure that has been rising through the 1990s. As the new century opens, the

FACING PAGE: *On a dairy farm and ranch near Baltic, hay rolls are loaded onto a flatbed. Dairy products are South Dakota's third leading livestock commodity.* BELOW: *There are five times as many cattle in South Dakota as there are people, a luxury of space that folks (and cows) in other states may well envy.*

state's primary and secondary producers annually generate wood products valued at nearly $177 million.

GOLD FEVER

The lure of gold had long been a factor in the exploration and development of what would become the Mount Rushmore State. Gold was finally discovered in the Black Hills in 1876, and the yellow ore has been coming out of that region's mines ever since. Today South Dakota is the nation's largest gold producer, helping to make the United States the second greatest producer in the world.

Virtually all gold mining is handled by four companies operating in the Black Hills: the Golden Reward Mine, Brohm Mining, Wharf Resources, and Homestake Mining Company. Homestake traces its history to the gold rush, and the Homestake Mine is the world's largest known deposit of iron-ore gold. Homestake has constructed the deepest underground mining operation in North America, descending to 8,000 feet. Since 1876 Homestake has prized more than 39 million ounces of gold from the earth, totalling more than $1 billion.

Together, the Black Hills mining companies produced almost 400,000 ounces of gold in 1998—representing a gross value of about $115 million. In some ways, the gold rush has never ended.

South Dakota, with granite and quartzite perhaps the most significant.

Eastern South Dakota is rich with rock deposits. The northeast is among the top three granite-mining areas in the country, yielding a unique, extremely hard, extremely consistent reddish stone valued in multiple applications.

Today two large operations dominate the granite industry: Cold Spring Granite and Dakota Granite. Both run quarries and fabrication facilities at Milbank. For much of the companies' histories, their bread and butter has been "monumental stone"—headstones, mausoleums, and so on—with architectural applications an important market for less than perfect stone. In later years, though, the two companies have found new applications. Today Cold Spring boasts of its expertise in custom fabrication, claiming the ability to meet virtually any need a customer may have. Dakota Granite is recognized as an industry leader in granite flooring, producing at least five different types of tile.

Between them, they also produce pillars and columns; landscape rocks and terracing stones; paving stones; granite signs; countertops; tabletops; and monuments and mausoleums, in any number of styles.

In the southeast the rock is quartzite, a highly variegated mineral ranging in color from pink to pink-gray. South Dakota quartzite has long been in high demand for railroads, bridges, and concrete construction because of its hardness and durability. In recent years it has become increasingly popular in building and landscaping, and quartzite mine operators such as L. G. Everist at Dell Rapids and Spencer Quarries at Spencer find themselves growing busier all the time, and not minding a bit.

Based in Rapid City, the state Stockgrowers Association is one of several South Dakota organizations that exist to promote the beef industry and to represent the interests of livestock growers at the state and national level.

ALL THAT GLITTERS IS NOT GOLD

Granite and quartzite, sand and gravel, and cement are second only to gold in economic importance here in

CHAPTER SEVENTEEN

GREAT TIMES, GREAT BUSINESS

Tourism is South Dakota's second most profitable industry. It is also the state's fastest growing sector and perhaps its most varied. The Mount Rushmore State offers awe-inspiring monuments and memorials, glitzy roadside attractions, scenic vistas and pellucid blue waters, casinos, nightclubs, and restaurants, all adding up to about $1 billion worth of economic activity every year and some 28,000 jobs—figures rising as the century turns.

JUST FACE IT

Mount Rushmore National Memorial claims center stage—and 2.7 million visitors annually. Fresh from a major renovation of parking, dining, and gift shop facilities, "the Faces" are probably the most recognized anthropoid monument in the country after the Statue of Liberty.

Nearby, the Crazy Horse Memorial puts a new face on the Black Hills. Still under construction after 50 years, Crazy Horse ultimately will dwarf Rushmore but will undoubtedly complement rather than compete with other Hills attractions.

The Hills themselves create some of the best draws: more than a dozen state and national parks, grasslands, forests, and memorials; more than one million acres of unadulterated beauty. Parts of Kevin Costner's *Dances with Wolves* were filmed here, in Spearfish Canyon. That must be when he fell in love with the Hills, prompting him and his brother Dan to build their famous Midnight Star casino in nearby Deadwood. That town, plus Lead, Custer, and other Old West sites, are tops on the "must-see" list.

NEXT STOP. . .

Ninety miles east, the White River Badlands spread 37 million years of prehistory before visitors—a good many of whom visit Wall Drug on the Badlands' northeastern

edge, or "wall." Wall Drug's fame began in the "dirty thirties," when the owners posted "free ice water" signs on the highway to attract parched motorists. It worked. Now as many as 20,000 visitors a day tour the city-block-sized complex of restaurants, western art gallery, and shops and emporiums. Ice water is still free.

Traveling east, one reaches the Missouri River and its Great Lakes of South Dakota. There are four man-made lakes from Pierre to Yankton, drawing anglers, boaters, hunters, campers, and other outdoors enthusiasts from everywhere. The smallest of these lakes, Lewis and Clark, laps up against the territorial capital, Yankton, a historic community whose riverside location has always made it important in transportation and whose curious blend of European village and prairie town is simply beautiful.

Equally attractive is Mitchell, home of the peculiarly appealing Moorish-style Corn Palace. This auditorium, conceived in 1892 to show off South Dakota products, is decorated annually with different varieties of maize as well as other grains and native grasses—to the tune of

Children enjoy one of several activity pools at Sioux Falls' Wild Water West. The park offers more than 50 acres of pools, water slides, go-cart tracks, miniature golf, and other family fun.

PHOTO: Courtesy, Wild Water West Waterpark & Family Amusement Park

Murdo's Pioneer Auto Museum and Antique Town houses more than 250 rare automobiles, including a Tucker, an Edsel, and various "muscle" cars of the 1950s and 1960s.

Sioux Falls, tourists almost invariably stop to shop at The Empire.

THIS PLACE IS A MEET MARKET

South Dakota attracts an increasing number of conventions and trade shows. Rapid City and Sioux Falls lead the way with their Rushmore Plaza Civic Center and Sioux Falls Arena and Convention Center, respectively.

Rushmore Plaza boasts 140,000 square feet of meeting and exhibit space, an 11,000-seat arena, a 1,789-seat theater, and 27 meeting rooms. It also hosts concerts and other live shows. Rapid City's scenic location, convenient air and ground access, and plentiful hotel rooms make it a key player in the convention trade.

Equally accessible is Sioux Falls. The 8000-seat Arena recently added a Sheraton convention facility with 100,000 square feet of meeting and exhibit space and a 16,000-square-foot ballroom. The city's central location, in proximity to two interstate highways, and major airport facility, including a U.S. Customs Port of Entry, all point to continued success well into the future.

about $100,000 every year. The Palace's boards have been trod by everyone from John Philip Sousa to Three Dog Night and many others.

WE GOT GAME!

Across the state, Indian reservations feature casinos and entertainment complexes, including the Sisseton-Wahpeton Dakota Oyate's Dakota Sioux, Dakota Connection, and Dakota Magic; and the Flandreau Santee Sioux tribe's Royal River Casino. Reservation gaming has emerged as an important tourism industry component. Reservations also offer other attractions, such as cultural and historical centers and powwows.

FOR ARTS' SAKE

In 1999 the South Dakota Arts Council awarded nearly $375,000 to individuals, organizations, and schools, supporting everything from South Dakota's several symphonies, including those in Rapid City and Sioux Falls, to a filmmaker's postproduction work.

SETTING UP SHOP

Finally, there's the place that some consider the state's biggest tourist attraction: The Empire/Empire East, a formidable mall of some 180 shops, restaurants, arcades, and kiosks, visited by 14 million folks a year. People may come to view Sioux Falls' namesake waterfalls, take in its Great Plains Zoo and Delbridge Museum, or see the au naturel splendor of the cast reproduction of Michelangelo's *David*. But whatever brings them to

MAN WITH A MISSION

The world's only Petrified Wood Park fills two blocks of downtown Lemmon with colorful towers, wishing wells, and castles—part of a 6.4 million-ton harvest of petrified logs and stumps found near the town in the 1930s by amateur geologist Ole Quammen.

Variety is a hallmark of the arts here. Larger communities have their symphonies and theaters, galleries and museums. But there are some delightfully unexpected treats found in smaller towns, such as the Shrine to Music Museum in Vermillion or the collection of plains literature and artifacts at the Center for Western Studies in Sioux Falls. There are dozens of others. Among the best known are the Redlin Art Center in Watertown; the Laura Ingalls Wilder Pageant at De Smet; the L. Frank Baum Festival at Aberdeen, where Baum lived before writing his first "Oz" book and where he is celebrated not only in the annual festival but also in a "Land of Oz" attraction at Storybook Land fantasy park; and the new Washington Pavilion of Arts and Science, expected to be Sioux Falls' cultural centerpiece. Housed in a historic former high school building, the pavilion features the 1,900-seat Great Hall and smaller performance spaces, the Kirby Science Discovery Center with its Wells Fargo CineDome Theater for 70-millimeter films, and the Visual Arts Center.

SPORTING CHANCES

Professional sports are fairly new here, but that doesn't dampen fans' enthusiasm. The Sioux Falls Canaries,

FACING PAGE: *The Missouri River runs the length of the state and offers fishing, swimming, wind-surfing, water skiing, and canoeing.*

Deadwood is a lot safer these days than in 1876, when Wild Bill Hickok was killed playing poker in a saloon. But you can still gamble here, and the restaurants and entertainment are better than ever.

reincarnation of an early twentieth-century baseball team, is a top-ranked member of the Northern League. The Sioux Falls Skyforce is one of the winningest teams in the Continental Basketball Association, which also includes the top-notch Rapid City Thrillers. And the Sioux Falls Stampede will bring hockey fans to the Sioux Falls Arena before the century turns.

That barely scratches the surface, of course. The Mount Rushmore State's attractions are by no means limited to big heads carved on mountaintops. But South Dakota's citizens are proud of those, too.

WHAT'S ALL THAT RUCKUS?

In April 1999 the South Dakota Symphony treated Sioux Falls elementary schoolchildren to a concert in the Great Hall of the not yet opened Washington Pavilion of Arts and Science. Before the performance, conductor Henry Charles Smith stood on stage and crumpled a dollar bill, asking the children in the last row of the highest balcony if they could hear it. They could.

PART FOUR

REFLECTIONS AND VISIONS

Innovation flows freely in this land renowned for the beauty and power of nature—a land that has inspired ordinary people to greatness for centuries. The Mount Rushmore National Memorial, the most recognized sculpture in the world, celebrates achievement and vision—yet embodies those very qualities itself. As more people are drawn to the state for a share of the inspiration, South Dakota has begun soul searching: How to create a brilliant future that retains the timelessness of community?

In the following pages leaders from a variety of economic sectors address this question, tying the advances of the twentieth century to the possibilities of the twenty-first. Just as the automobile and all-weather roadways, telephone, radio, and television profoundly impacted life in South Dakota earlier in the century, fiber optics, satellite communications, computerization, and the Internet are leading the charge at its close.

An outstanding quality of life will be integral to the state's successful future. South Dakotans recognize the importance of education to growth; technology facilitates the process. A new "covenant of trust" between employees and employers will become the foundation for a career-resilient workforce. And at the foundation of tomorrow is the preservation of clean water, blue skies, green grass, spacious living, and the cultural and artistic heritage of the people.

The Lakota Sioux believed that the spirits of their ancestors dwelled amid the lakes and forests of the majestic and serene Black Hills, and thus viewed this ancient land as sacred.

A PART OF ALL THAT WE ARE

JANET BROWN
Executive Director, South Dakotans for the Arts

A popular speaker on the influence of the arts on economic, cultural, and educational development, Janet Brown is executive director of South Dakotans for the Arts, South Dakota Community Arts Network, and South Dakota Alliance for Arts Education. She previously was one of the managers of Joseph Papp's New York Shakespeare Festival; she also managed the national tour of *The Pirates of Penzance* and the European tour of *Ain't Misbehavin'*. Brown was the first South Dakotan to serve on the board of directors of Americans for the Arts. She is currently treasurer of the United Statewide Community Arts Association and, among numerous other activities, has served as an on-site evaluator and panelist for the National Endowment for the Arts.

The history and landscape of South Dakota have inspired artists for centuries. South Dakota's rich heritage of Native American tribes and northern European settlers has been recorded and often romanticized by artists from Harvey Dunn to Yanktonai Sioux Oscar Howe. The arts in the early 1900s were defined by traveling chautauquas,

vaudeville shows, barn dances, and the determination of immigrants to keep their culture alive as they built a new life for themselves. The arts were a common attribute of everyday life; even Wild Bill Hickok played the violin. The arts were nurtured in one-room schoolhouses and homes, where storytelling, poetry, painting, and music were considered a necessary part of education.

Towns both large and small constructed opera and vaudeville houses that featured touring entertainers, most of whom arrived by rail. The restoration of these performing venues on the main streets of South Dakota communities has become a focal point today for a revival of performing arts and community pride.

PEOPLE OF VISION
At the time the arts of northern European settlers were taking hold in the state, the Native American tribes that

> THE LAKOTA, DAKOTA, AND NAKOTA TRIBES HAVE NO WORD FOR *ART*; IT IS SYNONYMOUS WITH WHAT IT MEANS TO BE HUMAN

had roamed Dakota Territory were being placed on reservations. The Lakota, Dakota, and Nakota Sioux tribes have no word for art because it is synonymous with what it means to be a human being. As the tribes began to assimilate into the white culture, there were those individuals who kept the songs, dances, and bead- and quillwork alive to pass on to future generations. Without these people of vision, South Dakota could have lost a precious part of its cultural heritage in the early part of the century. Today artwork of the Northern Plains Indians has become extremely popular, and many South Dakota Native American artists are finding success with both traditional and nontraditional art forms.

South Dakota is home to the most internationally recognized sculpture in the world: the massive carving of four American presidents on Mount Rushmore. Completed in 1941, Gutzon Borglum's "shrine of democracy" is visited by millions each year, and its positive impact on the economy of the state is unquestioned. In 1947 a second mountain sculpture, of the Lakota warrior Crazy Horse, was begun about twenty miles south of Mount Rushmore, near Custer, by Korczak Ziolkowski. Although the sculptor died in 1982, his wife, Ruth, and children carry on his work.

KEYS TO SUCCESS

In 1966 South Dakota took advantage of funds granted by the National Endowment for the Arts to create the South Dakota Arts Council (SDAC), an office of the South Dakota Department of Education and Cultural Affairs. In a state of only 750,000 people, government plays an enormous role in peoples' lives. Utilizing state, federal, and private funds, the SDAC has been a major factor in stabilizing arts institutions, encouraging arts education in our schools, and creating an environment beneficial to professional artists.

In the early years SDAC focused on establishing local arts councils in communities of all sizes. Today there are 48 active arts councils across the state, many serving multicity and -county regions. The strength of the state arts council has always been its democratic distribution of funds throughout South Dakota. Charlotte Carver, of Sioux Falls, the council's first executive director, deserves credit for sustaining SDAC from its inception in 1966 through to her retirement in 1988. The agency continues today under the experienced direction of Dennis Holub, a native South Dakotan who has been with SDAC since 1970.

As South Dakota enters the twenty-first century, cultural growth will become more critical to communities. Economic development and cultural development will go hand in hand. Communities will be successful by keeping their own identity, stressing their cultural and artistic heritage, and maintaining the beauty of their

Through his dance performance at one of the powwows held by the Lakota, Dakota, and Nakota tribes, a young Sioux helps keep South Dakota's rich cultural heritage alive for future generations.

surroundings. Artists have much to offer this transition into the new millennium.

South Dakota has artists who strive for excellence inspired by the vast openness of the prairie, the beauty of the Black Hills, and the integrity of all the peoples of the state. Professional writers, visual artists, musicians, actors, directors, and dancers join together with dedicated amateurs in a growing cultural awareness that art is part of all our lives, not just the lives of those who live in expensive houses in big cities. It is a part of who we are, like the land and history that define us.

TEAMING UP FOR A NEW FUTURE

KRISTINE MALLOY

South Dakota 1999 Teacher of the Year

Kristine Malloy, South Dakota's Teacher of the Year for 1999, teaches third grade at Parkston Elementary School. Prior to joining the Parkston team in 1991, she taught high school special education in the district for six years. Involving community members in the education system is one of the myriad secrets of her success. Malloy initiated the idea of a "math night" at school for students, parents, and local businesspeople, as well as the "grandteacher" program that brings retirees into the classroom. In 1995 she received the Presidential Award for Excellence in Science and Mathematics Teaching. Malloy holds both bachelor's and master's degrees from the University of South Dakota.

I would like to begin with the premise that standing in front of a classroom full of children is an enormous responsibility and privilege. What a teacher says and does can stay with a child for a lifetime. When I was assigned my first classroom 14 years ago, my philosophy of teaching was based on the formal models I studied in college. Today I feel we have seen some enormous changes in education.

After nearly a decade and a half in the field, I firmly believe that we need to look at education as a partnership between parents, schools, and businesses. Educators must be involved in the decision-making process, as must the community. The community is the glue that holds an effective school together. The enormity of the task of educating our children requires teamwork; we cannot afford to have people working in isolation.

We as educators must learn to help each other be right, rather than wrong, and to look for ways to make new ideas work, rather than for reasons they won't. We must speak positively about each other and about education at every opportunity. If we don't speak well of our profession, who will?

Furthermore, we need to work on creating an environment in which people are encouraged to take educated risks. Businesses believe that taking big risks is

> BUSINESSES BELIEVE THAT TAKING BIG RISKS ENSURES BIG RETURNS; THIS AXIOM HOLDS TRUE IN EDUCATION

the only way to ensure big returns; this axiom definitely holds true in education. We have to take risks in order to grow. If we stop growing, so will our students.

Teachers are team members with our students. We serve as their mentors. But to fulfill this essential role we must also be scholars, staying well informed and constantly becoming professionally renewed. To inspire students, we ourselves must be inspired.

AN ELECTRONIC WORLD

For success in the new millennium, we have to examine methods of effectively integrating technology into our classrooms. In recent years there has been a clear shift from the paper world to the electronic world. Almost every other enterprise in the country, from banks to airlines to hotels, has been transformed by technology. Companies simply could not carry on their work without it. Technological innovations come about so quickly, however, that many educators feel they lack the skills to keep up. In addition, our access to technology is inconsistent: some classrooms have it while others don't.

Putting computers in classrooms is only part of the task. The real value of technology in our schools depends on how fully it is integrated into the curriculum and, ultimately, how well teachers are prepared to use it. Most teachers are aware of the need to integrate technology into the existing curriculum, and most are struggling to accomplish it—but don't know where to start.

Our governor, William Janklow, has been instrumental in finding solutions to these challenges. A few years ago he initiated the wiring of all South Dakota schools for the Internet. He also established the Governor's Technology for Teaching and Learning Academy, an excellent professional development opportunity for teachers throughout the state. The teachers then return to their school districts and, in turn, share their newly acquired expertise with their colleagues. Professional development opportunities such as this are essential for educators to become comfortable with technology.

Furthermore, we need to create an environment in our schools and in the nation where shared expertise is a valued resource. When we break down the barriers between people, we can work as teams, respecting each other's opinions and points of view. I believe our nation has developed and thrived, and will continue to do so, through an intensive sharing of ideas.

PARADIGM SHIFT

We must change the paradigm in education that quality is controlled by the amount of money a school district has. Federal, state, and local agencies determine the amount of money given to a district; it can spend only what it is given or what it can raise through taxation. We can no longer rely on government for the funding of

A teacher and students explore an interactive Web site. With their school—and all South Dakota schools—wired for the Internet, these children will have an edge on success in the new millennium.

schools. If we are to control quality, then grants, profit centers, foundations, and cooperation between schools and businesses are necessary. Quality, rather than money, must drive the goal-setting process for schools. We must set our quality goals first, then find the money to accomplish them.

As a teacher, I have been given a most incredible, demanding, and overwhelming responsibility—and like many of us, I love it. The rewards do not come in public recognition, bonuses, promotions, or monetary awards. They come in the form of a thank-you note from a parent or the sparkle in the eye of a student grasping a new idea. These rewards will keep me teaching into the new millennium. The changes I hope to see—an inspired decision-making process, wholehearted teamwork, technologically integrated classrooms—will keep education meaningful in the years ahead.

GROWTH THROUGH CHANGE

ROBERT T. TAD PERRY

Executive Director, South Dakota Board of Regents

Robert T. Tad Perry became executive director for the South Dakota Board of Regents in 1994 following a 23-year career at Ball State University in Indiana. Dr. Perry was a faculty member and academic administrator before joining that university's central administration, where he rose to associate vice president. Immediately prior to moving to South Dakota, he was the chief operating officer for Indiana's Partnership for Statewide Education, a consortium of the state's public and independent institutions for delivering higher education through distance learning. His professional scholarship has focused on state government, public policy, and telecommunication applications in higher education.

As we embrace the new millennium, it is time to reflect on our past, our present, and our vision for the future.

The past century has held many changes for South Dakota higher education. These changes directly reflect the

needs of the people and the state. We place a high value on higher education in South Dakota because we

recognize its importance to growth. John F. Kennedy once said "Our progress as a nation can be no swifter than our progress in education."

Early South Dakotans recognized the importance of higher education and established the first university—the present-day University of South Dakota—at Vermillion in 1862, 27 years before the declaration of statehood. The Dakota Territory legislature showed its commitment to higher education again in 1881 when it approved a land-grant institution, South Dakota State University, in Brookings, to provide agricultural and mechanical education and a normal school, Black Hills State University, in Spearfish, to provide teacher training. Three other institutions were added in the 1880s, and the last at the turn of the century. The structure of higher education was set at that point.

The nature of higher education in the state, however, was shaped by world events. World War II and the Soviet

WORLD WAR II AND THE SOVIET LAUNCH OF SPUTNIK IN 1957 CREATED A NEED FOR SCIENTIFIC ADVANCEMENTS

launch of Sputnik in 1957 created a need for scientific advancements. In response, the South Dakota School of Mines and Technology expanded its mission, mining education, into other areas of science and technology. Following the implementation of the GI Bill, higher education throughout the state prepared for the needs of new people in the system. More housing, including married students' quarters, was built on campuses. When the reality of globalization of the marketplace came into view, South Dakota universities adjusted their curricula to prepare students for this new arena. Northern State University in Aberdeen added a program to train graduates in conducting business in an international environment.

RESTRUCTURING THE CURRICULA

Advancements in technology have impacted higher education in South Dakota just as they have elsewhere.

IN THE NEW ERA, TECHNOLOGY ADVANCES WILL MAKE IT POSSIBLE TO DELIVER NEEDED UNIVERSITY EDUCATION EVERYWHERE IN THE STATE

In answer to the workforce's technological needs, curricula have been restructured and new programs added. Perhaps the most significant response occurred in 1984, when Governor William Janklow closed the University of South Dakota at Springfield and created a new mission for Dakota State University in Madison to offer programs both for computer majors and for integrating computer technology into other areas of the curriculum.

At the close of the twentieth century, technology has revolutionized communications. Students having questions about an assignment can contact their teacher by E-mail. Communicating has become more convenient for both students and teachers since schedules do not have to be coordinated. In addition, teachers use the Internet to create Web sites on which they can post their class syllabus and assignments.

ON THE LEADING EDGE

Technology has dissolved the distance barrier for those who want to further their education. Using distance education technology, classes taught on university campuses can be broadcast to sites across the state. These classes can be interactive, so that each location can see and hear the other. Airing classes over local cable TV stations and South Dakota Public Broadcasting is another means for realizing distance education. Courses offered over the Internet are the newest advancement in this arena. College credit can be earned by anyone having access to a computer connected to the Internet, without stepping into a classroom. On-line classes not only dissolve the distance barrier but also the time barrier, because they can be taken any hour of the day or night, whenever the student has the inclination to log on.

The future of South Dakota higher education depends on the sector's ability to embrace change. The state's public universities are ready for this new millennium. In the closing years of the system's first century, numerous changes have taken place in preparation for the twenty-first century: a new approach to

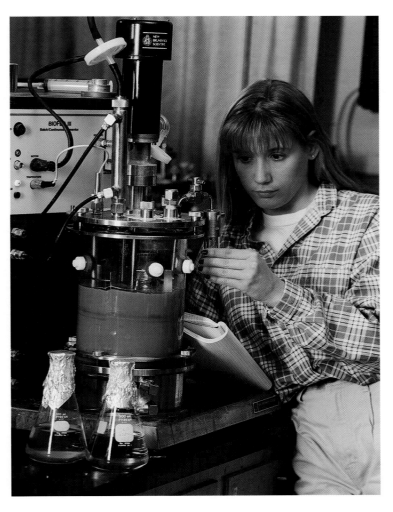

A university undergraduate researches compounds in the lab for her chemistry class. The opportunity for hands-on research was once open only to graduate students.

funding universities, with incentives for achieving state goals; an effort to make salaries more competitive as institutions attract and retain the best of faculty; the establishment of nine centers of academic excellence; and major investments in the applications of technology throughout the university curriculum. In the new era, lifelong learning will be the norm, and technology advances will make it possible to deliver needed university education everywhere in South Dakota.

Our universities are ready to meet the new expectations for convenient access for students bound by time and place demands. South Dakota's universities are ready to contribute as the state prepares for the next century.

THE CHANGING PRAIRIE

AELRED J. KURTENBACH

President and Chief Executive Officer, Daktronics, Inc.

Dr. Aelred J. Kurtenbach cofounded Daktronics, Inc., in 1968 while teaching electrical engineering at South Dakota State University. He has since served as CEO, president, and director of the company, which designs, manufactures, markets, and services large computer-programmable displays (primarily scoreboards) globally. Twice named South Dakota's Small Businessman of the Year, the Dimock, South Dakota, native currently serves as chairman of three entities: the education committee of the South Dakota Chamber of Commerce and Industry, the South Dakota District Export Council, and the South Dakota EPSCoR Committee, a program sponsored by the National Science Foundation.

The twentieth century was a period of tremendous change, with a profound impact on South Dakota. The automobile, the telephone, and the radio, followed by trucks and a usable road system, transformed rural life during the first half of the century. These innovations enabled the development of community among the dispersed farmsteads that existed at the start of the century because of the conditions in the Homestead Act, which allocated 160 acres of land to settlers who met certain improvement conditions.

Change did not slow during the second half of the century. Farmers wanted a better life for their children and stressed education as the means to achieve it. This desire of parents, coupled with tremendous increases in agricultural productivity, led to a trend of out-migration of our educated youth that was not reversed until the late 1980s.

Manufacturing had a short period of emphasis during the 1920s, primarily due to interest in better farm machinery and generally good economic times. The Great Depression of the 1930s stymied production agriculture in the state, along with most supporting business and industry, and effected another, greater out-migration from the state that continued for four decades.

> MANUFACTURING HAD A SHORT PERIOD OF EMPHASIS IN THE 1920S DUE TO INTEREST IN BETTER FARM MACHINERY

ONE BY ONE

Manufacturing activities started making rather isolated reappearances in the 1950s and 1960s. Raven Industries in Sioux Falls, led by Ed Owen, is the company that I recall. It started as primarily a contract manufacturer, and over time it has developed an extensive product line. During the late 1980s and 1990s other manufacturing companies, for the most part in communities along the interstate highways, became more prominent and employed more workers.

State government encouraged manufacturing companies to locate facilities in the state. During the 1980s the state also initiated programs to encourage the formation of start-up technology-based enterprises and to assist all manufacturing companies to increase employment inside the state.

Native American communities in South Dakota organized various manufacturing activities during the latter half of the century with limited success. (As the century closes, the gaming industry, which is legally allowed to locate on Indian reservations, is providing significant new opportunity for Native Americans. The cash flow from gaming, which is supplied primarily by non-Indians, is being used to secure better educational and economic opportunities for the state's Native Americans.)

The invention of the transistor at Bell Labs in New Jersey in the 1950s initially appeared to have little impact on the state. At the close of the century, however, the impact of the transistor and all of its follow-on products has been profound. Computers and communication systems based on solid-state technology are now in use throughout the state. Numerous companies are involved in electronics, computer, and communication manufacturing enterprises.

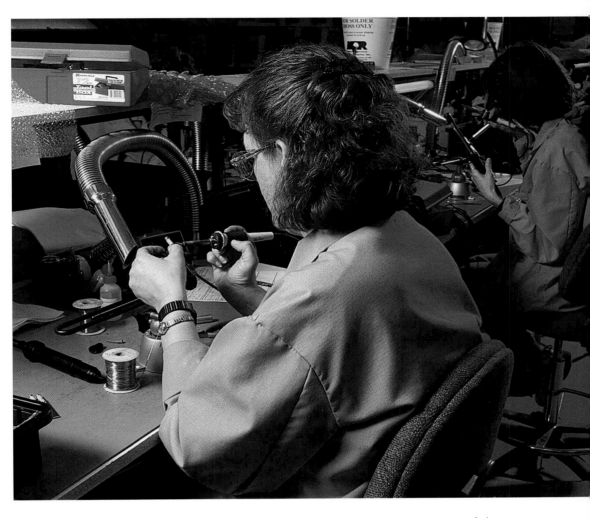

Assembly-line workers make electronic components, one of the state's many thriving manufacturing endeavors. Others include aerospace, computer, and telecommunications equipment.

Products manufactured in the state are shipped worldwide. Existing road systems encourage shipments north into Canada and south into Mexico. Excellent data communication systems enable the delivery of software products and data anywhere in the world.

ALL SYSTEMS GO

Opportunities in the twenty-first century abound for South Dakotans, because future economic growth is likely to be initiated, as it has been in the past, by innovative and technically active young people. Since the state's two engineering colleges are strategically situated in environmentally attractive settings, more

young people undoubtedly will opt to stay nearby after completing their studies. Their interest in and their need for continued educational activities throughout their lifetimes will be supported. Because South Dakotans are few but well educated, the state's manufacturing enterprises will tend to be smaller, with more specialized, higher value products. South Dakota's industrial activities of the twenty-first century will be enabled and enhanced by the state's interstate highway system, vastly improved communication systems based on optical fiber and satellite communication, and lifestyles involving clean water, blue skies, green grass, and spacious living.

A LEGACY WORTH OUR EFFORTS

NANCY EKSTRUM
Mayor of Philip

Nancy Ekstrum has called this small, rural community on the prairie home since 1946. Like many World War II veterans, her parents possessed the courage and daring to try something new. Despite the trials of locating in Philip, owning a hardware store, and raising six children, they succeeded enough to send Ekstrum to the University of South Dakota, where she earned a bachelor's degree in education. Graduation led to a teaching job in Las Vegas, Nevada—an exciting area, but one she found couldn't compete with South Dakota and her attachments here, especially to her future husband and the wide open spaces. Like her parents, she found the prairie to be a nurturing place to raise her two children.

I can't pinpoint when it began; it was an ever so subtle evolution. I stopped giving excuses for living in South Dakota. The transition may have begun when I realized that my California cousins thought it was cool to come to "Dakota" to spend summers fishing or playing baseball, no matter how good they were at the pastime or sport.

Or maybe it was when the foreign exchange student stood awestruck as she looked west at a sunset and exclaimed, "I have never seen the sun kiss the earth." Then again, my shift in attitude might have been caused by my daughter's reaction to a seminar she was to attend in Washington, D.C. She left Philip feeling somewhat apprehensive about whether she had the knowledge she would need to participate—and came home realizing that she had been able to compete quite easily with the urban students. But then, why should that come as a surprise? South Dakota students have always scored very well in academic testing.

CARING, PERSON TO PERSON

What is it about this rural state that keeps us here? Could it be the way entire towns keep track of their children? I remember the phone call from our local grocery store clerk alerting me to the fact that my 10-year-old son had been in trying to buy chewing tobacco. Or is it the concern we have for one another, illustrated, perhaps, by the fact that the other night I had dialed the wrong telephone number but continued to talk to the person for several minutes because her mother had been ill.

Without a doubt, however, the people who choose South Dakota as their home are the main reason we stay. South Dakotans are a hardy lot. We have to be. This sometimes harsh country demands that we be tenacious. We are accustomed to working for what we have and have little patience for those who don't. We are morally centered and still have the capacity to become enraged when we feel wrongs have been committed. We are generous with our time, talents, and efforts. There is a strong sense of self-reliance when it comes to solving problems, but there is a stronger desire to help others when situations arise that demand a community effort. You might say

> THERE IS A STRONG SENSE OF SELF-RELIANCE, BUT A STRONGER DESIRE TO HELP OTHERS WHEN THE NEED ARISES

we are a puzzlement. Rugged individualism does coexist with an intense sense of group.

SHARING THE WEALTH

The trend-studying people say that Americans are abandoning the cities for quality-of-life reasons: they want low crime rates, comparatively low housing costs, recreational opportunities, and, perhaps most of all, a return to community values. Each and every one of these qualities describes South Dakota. A potential influx of people, then, will be one of the challenges the leaders of South Dakota must address as we move into the next century.

We no longer feel the need to explain to people

Spearfish Canyon's rustic cabins, blue skies, and clean air symbolize South Dakota's outstanding quality of life, which is becoming more and more attractive to those outside the state.

why we live here. For many years we've worked to "sell" South Dakota, to be able to say "rural" with pride. Now we have a state that is on the threshold of change. I believe we will need to adopt a certain measuring stick to determine how selective we wish to be in allowing that image to change. How much of "rural" do we wish to preserve and how much of it do we want to share? Increasingly, our blue skies, clean air, honest people, and traditional values are becoming very attractive to others. They want what we have had for years. It will be our challenge to promote positive change so that we are able to preserve what we love about South Dakota and thereby leave a legacy worthy of our efforts.

The next step requires the arduous task of adopting a direction of development. I have not seen any printed plan as yet, but it surely becomes a topic of conversation

wherever small groups gather or when people talk about "progress." Nearly always we agree that we need to broaden our economic bases, but when we begin to discuss the price we might pay for "progress," internally we all begin prioritizing. And the hard questions arise: Will the activity leave our traditional values intact in the long term? Or are we looking at short-term gratification only? As we come to believe more and more in our own goodness and our own abilities to solve our problems, we will do what we have done for over a century: once we are committed to a task, we work hard, we work tenaciously, and we protect with a passion those things we value.

CELEBRATING A CENTURY

JERRY WHEELER

Executive Director and Chief Lobbyist, South Dakota Retailers Association
Jerry Wheeler's 30 years of experience in association management and legislative affairs have served him well—particularly since his 1990 appointment as executive director and chief lobbyist of the South Dakota Retailers Association, the oldest and one of the largest statewide retail associations in the nation. Prior to his work with the South Dakota Retailers Association, Wheeler was executive vice president of the South Dakota Automobile Dealers Association; executive director of the South Dakota Trucking Association; president and part owner of Capital Motors, Inc., in Pierre; and an accountant at a manufacturing firm.

The South Dakota Retailers Association celebrated its 100th anniversary in 1997. In conjunction with that milestone, we took a look back at not only our association's history but also at the history of retailing in South Dakota.

We were fascinated by the changes that had taken place in the retail sector over those 10 decades. We also discovered that many of the issues of concern today were likewise of concern a century ago.

A hundred years ago retailers served a small, agrarian population clustered in the eastern part of the state. There were predictions the area west of the Missouri River would never be settled.

> DIME STORE SUCCESS FORCED SMALL, INDEPENDENT MERCHANTS TO IMITATE THEIR WAY OF DOING BUSINESS

While that prediction proved untrue, today's merchants still market to a small population, and the retail sector remains very dependent on agriculture. When the farming community faces tough times, Main Street tightens its belt.

In the early days of retailing in South Dakota, most purchases were made on credit. For years there were heated arguments within the retail community as to whether or not it would be advantageous to eliminate credit and implement a cash-and-carry system.

Now a different form of credit reigns supreme: the credit card. The prevalence of easy credit has paved the way for other changes. Impulse buying is commonplace, and items that were considered luxuries only a few decades ago have become necessities today, simply because credit allows people to buy more.

Throughout the 1900s most small-town, independent merchants considered catalog companies to be their greatest competition. In the early part of the century, the South Dakota Retailers Association publicly referred to mail-order companies as parasites, pirates, and even homicidal organizations. Members of the association vowed not to do business with anyone who also did business with catalog companies.

CATALOGING THE CHANGES

Although retailers hoped that catalog buying would go out of vogue, catalog companies continued to flourish, offering the consuming public convenience and variety. The demand for both led to a revolution in retailing. Dime stores began to dot the landscape, followed by chain stores and franchises. Their success forced small, independent merchants to imitate their way of doing business. Good selection, good value, and good service became key elements of every business.

The newest form of competition, of course, is the Internet. While its impact is just starting to be felt, the Internet is bringing about a new wave of change in retailing. Already entrepreneurs are setting up shop on line, rather than investing in brick and mortar. Others are finding it profitable to do both, using the Internet to turn their little South Dakota businesses into global enterprises.

Other changes in technology also had an enormous impact on retailing. Life changed dramatically with the electrification of South Dakota in the 1930s and 1940s. The advent of radio and television provided new ways to market businesses and showed consumers how other people live, creating demand for a wider range of products and services. Computerization made inventory control more efficient.

The single greatest impact on retailing in our state, however, may have been the automobile.

ON THE ROAD

In 1900 there were 8,000 automobiles registered in the entire United States and only about 10 miles of paved road for them to travel on. Now, of course, most families own two cars, and the highway and a credit card will take them wherever their hearts desire.

The potential of the automobile was recognized early on by merchants. In a speech at our association's 1916 convention, one business owner stated, "Too much emphasis cannot be laid on the development of the out-of-town auto business. The increasing number of autos is one of the most helpful signs to us that there is prosperity ahead."

Mobility has caused changes in where we live and where we buy. A trip to the store used to be a major

Good selection, good value, and good service are the key elements of a successful business, whether a brick-and-mortar shop like these in downtown Brookings or a virtual shop on the Internet.

event. Now people think nothing of getting in the car and driving several hours to go shopping. Consequently, both our population and our retail centers are becoming concentrated in cities along the interstate highways.

When celebrating our association's centennial, we honored dozens of retail businesses throughout the state that also had survived more than a century. To stay in business that long takes determination and fortitude. Our state has plenty of both. So whatever the twenty-first century brings, we predict a bright future for retailing in South Dakota.

DEVELOPING CAREER RESILIENCE

TERRY SULLIVAN

Director, Southeast Technical Institute

Terry Sullivan has been director of Southeast Technical Institute, in Sioux Falls, since 1986. He currently oversees the development and construction of the institute's 165-acre campus, located on the northwest side of Sioux Falls. Sullivan was instrumental in obtaining the necessary legislature approvals for South Dakota's technical institutes to grant associate degrees. He has served on numerous boards and task forces and has written articles for many different publications, including the *Community College Journal*. He currently is a member of the board of directors of the Sioux Falls Area Chamber of Commerce and an executive committee member of the Forward Sioux Falls Workforce Development Council.

How many of us are old enough to remember what leisure life was like before television? I can recall in the 1950s joining some neighborhood kids on hot summer nights to watch this wonderfully exciting new entertainment invention through a store window; the shop owner was kind enough to leave the set playing until 10 p.m. each evening. Characters came to life on that black-and-white screen, and we kids were transported each night to places we never dreamed of or imagined before. We were filled with wonderment. What could ever top this? Then some years later came color television as well as myriad other technological inventions and discoveries that have made life so much more enjoyable for us. As a society, we have come to expect these enhancements.

Many years later, while interviewing for my present position and touring the old facilities of the institution that I now lead, I noted the sleek, streamlined IBM Selectric typewriters that were at that time a formidable part of the secretarial training program. I also noticed, over in the corner, new first-generation personal computers that were not getting much attention—but that eventually would not only revolutionize learning but also inextricably alter the nature of the workplace.

WHAT NEEDS TO BE FURTHER DEVELOPED BETWEEN EMPLOYER AND EMPLOYEE IS A COVENANT OF TRUST

I wonder, now, if I recognized then that we were leaving the industrial age and moving into the information age with the advent of these high-performance PCs. And as technology has moved us forward even beyond the information age to what we now call the knowledge age, do we know if we are prepared for this next surge as we speed toward a new millennium and all that it will offer?

NEW DEMANDS, NEW RESPONSES

As educators, how will we cope with the new demands placed upon our institutions for training and educating tomorrow's workforce? Are we changing appropriately and quickly enough to adjust to this accelerating rhythm?

Arguably, traditional forms of education do not provide the best preparation for our emerging economy. Vocational education has tended to become too focused on specific skills and occupations that are likely to change in the future. Academic education by itself is also inadequate because it does not equip students to apply their abstract knowledge to practical, problem-solving situations.

Meanwhile, employment is becoming increasingly fluid as occupational boundaries and company loyalties change or dissolve. Continuous learning is becoming a mainstay of the workplace because organizations are giving more responsibility to front-line staff for problem solving and improving procedures. Employees are obliged to move from one employer to another due to plant closings or major restructuring.

What needs to be further developed between employer and employee is a covenant of trust, with each performing an integral role: one providing training, the other participating in growth activities. Such a covenant inevitably will lead to a career-resilient workforce. This workforce will then look forward to change as a friend—not something to be feared, but rather to be welcomed as the inevitable result of technological innovations provided and accommodated for by talented and skilled workers.

With the help of the Internet, an academic student learns to apply her abstract knowledge to practical, problem-solving solutions— a critical skill for maneuvering in the emerging economy.

EVANGELISTS FOR THE DREAM

To assist in accomplishing this new strategy, which will enhance the ability of our workforce to become career resilient, educators and employees need to become evangelists for this dream. Employers and educators must work together to implement new workplace systems that address the education and training needs of South Dakota's workforce. For example, programs and curricula should be reviewed to integrate vocational and academic studies. Standards that represent both occupational and educational performance should be established to reflect mastery of the material. Education and training should include elements of work-based learning to prepare students for contextual learning applications. These are vital steps if education is to renew itself to meet workplace needs.

At the dawn of a new millennium, South Dakota's technical institutes are well positioned to serve as key providers of academic and occupational education for adults of all ages. They have been adaptive organizations that have fulfilled an array of needs directly related to the future growth and prosperity of South Dakota. Their expectations will continue to expand as they further develop strategic alliances with business and industry to help fulfill recurring workforce needs.

The challenges will be significant. Meeting the educational needs of an increasingly diverse population will be at the forefront. Extending our role as leaders in workforce training development will require diligence. And finally, developing flexible modes of instruction to continue to provide academic and occupational skills needed by adults and young people alike in a rural setting will provide both challenges and opportunities for all who wish to develop educational lifelines to the publics we serve.

TOURISM

PROGRESS, THE NATURAL WAY

PATRICIA RAHJA VAN GERPEN
Cabinet Secretary, South Dakota Department of Tourism
Patricia Van Gerpen began her career in government with the South Dakota Department of Tourism and the Governor's Office of Economic Development in 1983. After serving in various positions and finally as creative director for both offices, she was appointed secretary of the department of tourism in 1995. As such, she oversees all department operations and staff and manages a budget of $5.5 million. Van Gerpen works closely with the Visitor Industry Alliance (VIA), a statewide group of travel industry leaders, on legislation and issues facing the industry. She is a member of the VIA, the National Council of State Travel Directors, Travel Industry Association of America, the Travel and Tourism Research Association, CenStates Travel Research Association, and several local organizations.

South Dakota's tourism sector came into being in this century. The state's most significant visitor site, Mount Rushmore National Memorial, was completed in 1941. Sculptor Gutzon Borglum carved the faces of presidents George Washington, Thomas Jefferson, Teddy Roosevelt, and Abraham Lincoln in stone as the nation's

"shrine of democracy." The sculpture now draws 2.7 million visitors a year.

And the mountain carving in this state continues with Crazy Horse Memorial, which was begun in 1948. Sculptor Korczak Ziolkowski, who had worked with Borglum on Rushmore, was asked by Lakota chief Henry Standing Bear to carve this tribute to Lakota chief Crazy Horse "so that the white man may know that the red man has great heroes too." Visitors to the memorial today see history being made before their eyes as the carving continues, led by Ruth Ziolkowski, the sculptor's widow, and other family members.

CONTINUOUS EXPANSION
Most of the state's other major visitor attractions were created or developed within this century as well, from the Redlin Art Center and Falls Park to Fort Sisseton

PRESIDENT CALVIN COOLIDGE MADE CUSTER STATE PARK FAMOUS AS HIS SUMMER WHITE HOUSE IN 1927

and Badlands National Park. And the progress hasn't stopped. These attractions continue to grow and expand.

Several individuals influenced the state's travel industry significantly during the 1800s and 1900s in addition to Crazy Horse, Standing Bear, Borglum, and Ziolkowski. Explorers Lewis and Clark made their highway, the Missouri River, a visitor attraction. Wild Bill Hickok, Poker Alice, Calamity Jane, and Jack McCall made the historic town of Deadwood famous. L. Frank Baum, author of *The Wonderful Wizard of Oz*, left his mark on the town of Aberdeen. Laura Ingalls Wilder made the town of De Smet an attraction after writing *Little Town on the Prairie*. President Calvin Coolidge made Custer State Park famous by declaring its State Game Lodge his summer White House for the 1927 season. Wall Drug owners Ted and Dorothy Hustead created a winning marketing concept—free ice water for their customers—in the 1930s, turning their modest establishment into a

14-store shopping emporium. Wildlife and Americana painter Terry Redlin, named America's Most Popular Artist by *U.S. Art* magazine eight years running (1991–1998), created the Redlin Art Center.

As more and more people learn about and want to seek out the history of the Wild West and its pioneers, visitors to South Dakota now come from throughout the world—particularly the United Kingdom, Germany, France, and Japan. This sparsely populated state does not spend a great sum of money promoting its attractions domestically or internationally, yet it draws visitors from half a world away. The promotion of South Dakota tourism has changed dramatically from the early days, when no tourism organization existed anywhere in the state, to today, when four such groups are in place and aggressively promoting the destinations, along with numerous special interest organizations such as the Visitor Industry Alliance, Alliance of Tribal Tourism Advocates, Innkeepers Association, and others. The World Wide Web daily brings in hundreds of requests for information and dispenses travel information on the state to surfers everywhere.

After a little practice, these wanna-be cowboys are right at home on the range. Later they'll enjoy a chuck wagon supper by a campfire and sleep under the stars as part of their western adventure.

LOOKING AHEAD, SOUTH DAKOTA–STYLE

Change will continue to be a part of South Dakota's travel industry as more attractions, from archaeological digs to building restorations and historic parks, are being developed as spin-offs of the state's rich history. Because our state is not that old, its past is still being discovered and developed. This will continue in the twenty-first century, and the marketing of our attractions will become more sophisticated.

Looking ahead, I see more interest in U.S. history. Teachers and students will yearn to learn more about the early days of our country, which will point them in the direction of our earliest leaders—whose faces are carved in granite in our state. They will want to know more about South Dakota's American Indian people—the Lakota, Nakota, and Dakota—and their cultures. The explorations of Lewis and Clark will become a focal point, leading travelers to the lands these adventurers sought in the early 1800s. All of this interest will encourage South Dakota's travel industry leaders to find ways to develop sites that relate to this significant history, along with the infrastructure they require.

Leaders in the travel industry need to proceed cautiously with these developments so as not to lose sight of our beloved lifestyle. Development should be well thought out, with quality as the top priority. Historic preservation will become more critical for South Dakotans as more and more of us realize that we live next door to history. The appropriate and careful preservation of our state's attractions will be our pipeline to success, both as an industry and as a destination maintaining an enviable lifestyle.

PHOTO: © *South Dakota Tourism*

AN ERA ON THE MOVE

RON WHEELER

Secretary of the South Dakota Department of Transportation
Commissioner of the Governor's Office of Economic Development

After chairing a citizens' task force on the department of transportation at Governor William Janklow's request, Ron Wheeler was appointed secretary of the department in 1996 to implement the task force recommendations. A year later the governor expanded Wheeler's duties to include serving as commissioner of the office of economic development. Prior to his work in government, Wheeler was divisional president of U.K.–based Simon Engineering. There he managed eight companies around the world, including Simon-Telelect in Watertown and Huron, where he had worked his way up to the positions of president and chief executive officer.

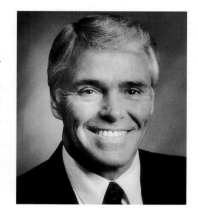

Significant transportation changes have taken place in South Dakota over the last 100 years. The most notable shift is that railroad transportation, which was dominant early in the century, has been replaced by highway transportation as the era comes to a close.

Railroads reached their peak in South Dakota in 1911. They carried immigrants into the state and agricultural products out of it. The presence of railroads often determined whether or not a community in the state would survive and prosper. A total of 4,420 miles of railroad track was constructed in South Dakota; operating trackage in the state today totals 1,855 miles.

THE PRESENCE OF RAILROADS OFTEN DETERMINED WHETHER A COMMUNITY WOULD SURVIVE AND PROSPER

The ebb of the railroads in South Dakota is based on several factors. Among them, declining customer service and the invention of the automobile—combined with the ability to mass-produce it—changed the face of transportation in South Dakota forever. With cars and trucks, businesses and people were no longer dependent on the train schedule to determine when they could move across the state. In addition, the replacement of dirt roads with all-weather roads helped the trucking industry compete with the railroads.

HIGHWAYS ON THE RISE

The construction of all-weather roads in South Dakota was impacted by two key events. The first occurred in the 1890s, when the U.S. Post Office decided to provide free rural delivery (FRD) on the condition that rural areas have all-weather roads. The second key event was in 1916, when Congress passed legislation authorizing federal funds to be matched with state funds for the construction of a highway system in each state. Under the new law the federal highway funds were distributed to each state according to a formula with factors of one-third population, one-third land area, and one-third postal miles. Each state had to create a highway department to receive federal funds. In 1917 South Dakota created the State Highway Department, which in 1973 became the South Dakota Department of Transportation.

To match the federal funds, South Dakota adopted a one-cent-per-gallon gasoline tax in 1921. In 1939 the state constitution was amended to insure that monies collected by the gas tax from highway use would be spent only on the construction and maintenance of highways.

President Dwight D. Eisenhower saw the need for a system of highways that would connect the states to provide for the easy flow of goods and people. He wanted it to support our nation's defense and promote economic prosperity. However, he envisioned developing a method to ensure continuing funds for the system without creating a huge national debt. The Federal Highway Act of 1956 provided for a 40,920-mile system of interstate and defense highways, the federal share of which would be 90 percent. To help fund the system on an ongoing basis, the bill also created a Highway Trust Fund for gas taxes paid by highway users. Federal highway allocations were not to exceed the balance of the trust fund.

South Dakota's two U.S. senators, Karl Mundt and Francis Case, were influential in designating the interstate highway routes through the state. Like the site selection for the railroads earlier in South Dakota's history, the siting of the interstate highways would have a significant positive impact on progressive communities situated along the routes. The final decision was to construct an east-west route, Interstate 90, to closely parallel pre-interstate U.S. Highway 16 and a north-south route, I-29, to parallel pre-interstate U.S. Highway 77 in eastern South Dakota. Construction began in Sioux Falls in 1955, although most of the system was built in the 1960s. The interstate system in South Dakota was completed in 1983, when the final segment of I-29 was opened to traffic near the town of Peever. Today there are 678 miles of interstate highway in South Dakota.

Open road and blue skies are the order of the day for the Badlands, shown here, as well as for much of the state. Conditions are generally ideal for transporting agricultural and other commodities.

BALANCING FUTURE NEEDS

Although it is difficult to predict the impact of new technologies and unforeseen inventions, in the future highway traffic growth will level off. Improvements in communications and the growth of the Internet will reduce the need for business travel. Agricultural products will continue to be the dominant commodities transported. However, there will be continued growth in the overnight package-delivery business. This will require increased investment in air freight facilities.

South Dakota has a very efficient transportation system that enables goods produced here to quickly reach the global marketplace. The citizens of South Dakota have made a huge investment in the transportation infrastructure, and it is the responsibility of future leaders and all South Dakotans to preserve and build upon it.

BIBLIOGRAPHY

Aberdeen Convention & Visitors Bureau. *Discover the Magic.* Aberdeen, S.Dak.: Aberdeen Convention & Visitors Bureau, 1998.

"Across the USA: News From Every State—South Dakota." In *Realty Times* [Web site] [cited 14 May 1999]. Available from www.realtytimes.com/rtnews/rtipages/19980714_ibuzz.htm#story3; INTERNET.

"America's 100 Most Wired Colleges." In *Y-Life* [Web site] [cited 1 April 1999]. Available from www.zdnet.com/yil/content/college/colleges98/surprise3.html; INTERNET.

American Automobile Association. *North Central Tour Book.* Heathrow, Fla.: AAA Publishing, 1998.

Black Hills, Badlands & Lakes Association. *Exploring the Black Hills and Badlands.* Rapid City, S. Dak.: Black Hills, Badlands & Lakes Association, 1998.

Black Hills Forest Resource Association. *A Century of Black Hills Silviculture.* Rapid City, S. Dak.: Black Hills Forest Resource Association, 1997.

———. *Black Hills Forest Products Industry.* Rapid City: Black Hills Forest Resource Association, 1997.

———. *The First Timber Sale: A Brief History of Case No. 1, Black Hills National Forest, South Dakota.* Rapid City: Black Hills Forest Resource Association. Undated.

———. *Logging in Western South Dakota.* Lead, S. Dak.: Historical Footprints, 1995. Videotape.

Boone, C. F. *The Rapid City Flood.* Lubbock, Tex.: C. F. Boone, 1972.

Brookings Convention & Visitors Bureau. *Brookings Visitor's Guide.* Brookings, S. Dak.: Brookings Convention & Visitors Bureau, 1998.

Childs, Marquis W. *Yesterday, Today, and Tomorrow: The Farmer Takes a Hand.* Washington, D.C.: National Rural Electric Cooperative Association, 1980.

Clow, Richmond L. "Timber Users, Timber Savers: Homestake Mining Company and the First Regulated Timber Harvest." *Forest History Today,* 1998.

Collier's Encyclopedia. New York: Macmillan Educational, 1990, s.v. "farm machinery."

Dedrick, Dave. *It Ain't All Cartoons.* Huron, S. Dak. : East Eagle Co., 1989.

Dewald, Mata, ed. *This Is South Dakota.* Rapid City, S.Dak.: Terrell Publishing, 1995.

Fradin, Dennis Brindell and Judith Bloom Fradin. *From Sea to Shining Sea: South Dakota.* Chicago: Children's Press, 1995.

Franklin, Dr. Douglas and Abdirizak Ahmed. "Farm Management Innovators: Characteristics of Eastern SD Farm Operators." *Economic Research Report 92-3.* Brookings, S. Dak.: South Dakota State University, 1992.

Froiland, Sven G. *Natural History of the Black Hills and Badlands.* Sioux Falls, S. Dak.: The Center for Western Studies, 1990.

Glacial Lakes & Prairies Tourism Association. *South Dakota Glacial Lakes & Prairies Regional Visitor's Guide.* Watertown, S. Dak.: Glacial Lakes & Prairies Tourism Association, 1998.

Great Lakes of South Dakota Association. *South Dakota Great Lakes 1998 Guide Along the Missouri River.* Pierre, S. Dak.: Great Lakes of South Dakota Association, 1998.

Griffith, Tom. *South Dakota.* 2nd ed. Compass American Guides. Oakland, Calif.: Fodor's Travel Publications, 1998.

Hasselstrom, Linda M. *Roadside History of South Dakota.* Missoula, Mont.: Mountain Press, 1994.

Hogan, Edward Patrick. *The Geography of South Dakota.* Sioux Falls, S. Dak.: Center for Western Studies, 1995.

———. *South Dakota: An Illustrated Geography.* Huron, S. Dak.: East Eagle, 1991.

Hogan, Edward Patrick, Lee A. Opheim, and Scott H. Zieske, eds. *Atlas of South Dakota.* Dubuque, Iowa.: Kendall/Hunt, 1970.

Hovey, Kendra A. and Harold A Hovey. *CQ's State Fact Finder.* Washington, D.C.: Congressional Quarterly, 1998.

Information Please [encyclopedia on-line], 1997, s. v. "South Dakota."

Kane, Joseph Nathan. *Famous First Facts.* 4th ed. New York: H. W. Wilson, 1981.

Karolevitz, Robert F. *Challenge: The South Dakota Story.* Sioux Falls, S. Dak.: Brevet Press, 1975.

Karolevitz, Robert F. and Bernie Hunhoff. *Uniquely South Dakota.* Norfolk, Va.: Donning, 1988.

"A Letter from the Editor." In South Dakota Magazine [Web site], 27 April 1999. Available from www.mainstreetweb.com/sdmagsample/; INTERNET.

Linde, Martha. *Sawmills of the Black Hills.* Rapid City, S. Dak.: Fenske Printing, 1984.

McCaig, Barbara and Lynn D. Soli. *South Dakota Recreation Guide.* Aberdeen, S.Dak.: Tensleep Publications, 1985.

McMacken, Robin. *The Dakotas: Off the Beaten Path.* Saybrook, Conn.: Globe Pequot Press, 1996.

Milton, John R. *South Dakota: A Bicentennial History.* New York: Norton, 1977.

Mobil Oil Co. *Mobil Travel Guide: Northwest and Great Plains.* New York: Prentice Hall, 1997.

"1999 College Rankings." In *U.S. News Online* [Web site], 3 October 1998. Available from www.usnews.com/usnews/edu/ugrad98; INTERNET.

Norris, Kathleen. *Dakota: A Spiritual Geography.* New York: Ticknor & Fields, 1993.

"Nouveau Frontier." In *BUILDER Online,* December 1998. Available from www.builder.hw.net; INTERNET.

Progulske, Donald R. and Richard H. Sowell. *Yellow Ore, Yellow Hair, Yellow Pine: A Photographic Study of a Century of Forest Ecology.* Brookings, S. Dak.: Agricultural Experiment Station, South Dakota State University, 1974.

Reynolds, William J. *Sioux Falls: The City and the People.* Helena, Mont.: American & World Geographic, 1994.

Sioux Falls Argus Leader. *The Argus Leader South Dakota 99.* Sioux Falls, S. Dak.: Ex Machina Pub. Co., 1989.

"Six South Dakota High Schools Among Most Wired." *Sioux Falls Argus Leader,* 4 April 1999.

Smith, Rex Alan. *The Carving of Mount Rushmore.* New York: Abbeville Press, 1985.

South Dakota Department of Tourism, et al. *South Dakota Vacation Guide 1998–1999.* Pierre, S. Dak.: South Dakota Department of Tourism, 1998.

South Dakota Division of Parks and Recreation. *South Dakota Park Times.* Pierre, S. Dak.: South Dakota Department of Game, Fish and Parks, 1998.

Swenson, Rob. "$44 Million Ethanol Plant Planned." *Sioux Falls Argus Leader,* 24 March 1999.

Vexler, Robert I., ed. *Chronology and Documentary Handbook of the State of South Dakota.* Dobbs Ferry, N.Y.: Oceana Publications, 1979.

Walker, Carson. "Logging Is Gold to Black Hills." *Sioux Falls Argus Leader,* 9 June 1992.

Winckler, Suzanne. *The Smithsonian Guides to Historic America: The Plains States.* New York: Stewart, Tabori & Chang, 1998.

Woster, Kevin. "The Missouri: Largest Reservoir System in North America." *Sioux Falls Argus Leader,* 16 May 1999.

Young, Steve. "Some Styles Try to Be People-Friendly." *Sioux Falls Argus Leader,* 31 May 1999.

In addition to the sources listed above, Web site postings by the following entities provided information used in this publication: Avera Health; Big Stone Lake Area Chamber of Commerce; Bizsites; Black Hills Information; Children's Care Hospital & School; Cold Springs Granite; DAKOTACARE; Dakota Dunes; Dakota Granite Company; Dakota, Minnesota & Eastern Railroad Corporation; Dakota State University; Daktronics, Inc.; The Deadwood Page; Federal Reserve Bank of Minneapolis; Forward Sioux Falls—Into the Next Century; Gateway; Geo-Heat Center; The Gold Institute; Green Tree Financial Services; Hieros Gamos—The Comprehensive Legal Site; Homestake Mining Company; Hutchinson Technology Incorporated; Joint Venture Project; LodgeNet Entertainment Corporation; Midcontinent Media; Midland National Life Insurance Company; Mining Matters—South Dakota; The Mortgage Mart; National Park Service; Quartzite Rock Association; Rapid City Regional Hospital; Roadside America; The Rough Guide Online; Sencore, Inc.; Sioux Falls Regional Airport; Sioux Valley Hospitals & Health System; Snowbear's Home Page; South Dakota Broadcasters Association; South Dakota Corn Utilization Council; South Dakota Department of Education and Cultural Affairs; South Dakota Department of Environment and Natural Resources; South Dakota Department of Labor; South Dakota Department of Transportation; South Dakota Governor's Office of Economic Development; South Dakota Home Page; South Dakota Newspaper Association; South Dakota Port USA; South Dakota Public Broadcasting; South Dakota Public Utilities Commission; South Dakota State Historical Society; South Dakota Telemedicine; South Dakota Tourism; Spearfish, South Dakota; University of South Dakota School of Law; SPS Payment Services, Inc.; U.S. Census Bureau; The U.S. Housing Markets; Vance Thompson M.D.; Wall Drug; Western Surety Company; WNAX.

INDEX